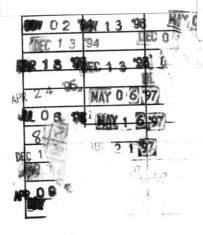

Death Row

Interviews with Inmates,
Their Families and
Opponents of Capital Punishment

by
Shirley Dicks

McFarland & Company, Inc., Publishers
Jefferson, North Carolina, and London

British Cataloguing-in-Publication data are available

Library of Congress Cataloguing-in-Publication Data

Death Row.
    [Includes index.]
    Includes bibliographical references.
    1. Capital punishment—United States. 2. Death
Row—United States—Case studies. 3. Prisoners—United
States—Biography. 4. Prisoners' families—United
States—Biography. I. Dicks, Shirley, 1940–
HV8699.U5D43   1990   364.6′6   89-13931

ISBN 0-89950-477-9 (sewn softcover; 55# alk. paper) ∞

Manufactured in the United States of America

McFarland & Company, Inc., Publishers
  Box 611, Jefferson, North Carolina 28640

This book is dedicated
with love to my son,
Jeff Dicks.
He sits on Tennessee's death row,
innocent of the crime
for which he was convicted.

Acknowledgments

I would like to thank all those people who gave me interviews and made this book possible.

I would like to thank especially the men on death row who have helped me by providing an inside glance into their daily lives.

To all the family members of those on death row, who gave a painful insight into their lives: It is my hope this book will let the people know about capital punishment and how unfair it is.

Table of Contents

Preface

This is a book about capital punishment. It is written in three parts. Part I deals with the people who fight against the death sentence. A few of them are:

Joe Ingle, who has been considered for the Nobel Peace Prize for his fight against capital punishment, tells how he became involved in trying to stop the death sentence. Joe has visited most of the death rows across the United States and met hundreds of the men housed there. He was with many of them during their last few hours on earth and ministered to their needs.

Watt Espy tells about his findings on the more than 15,000 executions that he has documented over the past 17 years. He has spent a lifetime chronicling every legal execution that has taken place in the United States since colonial times. "With every execution I feel a part of me dies," he says.

Richard Moran is a professor of sociology at Mt. Holyoke College and has written on the financial cost of capital punishment.

Patricia Smith was clemency attorney for Jerome Bowden, a retarded black man executed in Georgia.

Part II deals with the inmates themselves. They tell their stories truthfully and with remorse. Some are probably innocent of the crime for which they were convicted, and hope for relief in the state appeals process. All are poor and some come from broken homes and were abused as children. Nearly all had court-appointed attorneys who were overworked and underpaid.

Part III deals with the families of the condemned inmates. They tell of the pain and heartbreak they have gone through since their loved one was sentenced to die. The public sometimes treats them as if they also were behind bars, which means as if they were less than human.

I feel that this book is overdue. These are the unvarnished words of many kinds of people; all tell how wrong capital punishment is. The readers may make their own judgments. It is often said that innocent men have been unjustly sentenced to death; perhaps by the publication of this book, other cases not yet fatally and finally resolved can be brought to the public's attention. *All* death row cases invite a closer inspection.

Shirley Dicks
Murfreesboro, Tennessee
Fall 1989

Part I. Fighting the Death Penalty

Joe Ingle

Joe was considered for the Nobel Peace Prize in 1988 for his work against the death penalty. Much of the rest of the world opposes this barbaric American rite. No country in the Western alliance, except the United States, kills its own citizens. We are always talking about what champions we are of human rights and then we have this murder by the state. Europeans think we are hypocritical.

Joe says, "What's important is not so much Joe Ingle as what I symbolize to them, a struggle to end this society's practice of killing people."

"Joe Ingle's activities have opened the eyes of many people and changed public opinion," said Karin Soeder, a representative for the Swedish Center Party and one of those who submitted his name to the Nobel committee. "The death penalty is something we are following in every part of the world."

No one knows better than Joe Ingle that his ministry is unpopular with many people. His crusade is often a lonely one, depending in large part on inner strength. Perhaps this latest recognition and honor will renew his resolve and his hope.

"My personal interest in prisons began when I was in seminary in New York. I was just a white boy up from North Carolina and I didn't know anything about prisons when I heard about the uprising in Attica. I was reading in the *New York Times* about these guys who were angry about the conditions they were in and had control of the prison. I could see where all this was heading, for Governor Rockefeller was taking a very hard line. Sure enough he sent in the highway patrol and over forty people were killed. And interestingly enough when you look at who was killed and who did the killing, both prisoners and guards were killed but they were all killed by the troops who were sent in.

"The prisoners didn't kill any of the hostages and it seems to me they

1

conducted themselves rationally. They were very angry over the conditions that they were living in, and they were very responsible over what they were talking about but the Governor just exterminated them and took the prison.

"I started to visit the Bronx House of Detention, which is a big jail for the Bronx. I went up there for the first time and I'll never forget it. The guard took me to the cell block and opened the door. He slammed the door behind me. The first thought I had was, oh my God, he's locked me in here with all these animals. I started talking to them and I learned a lot. I learned that we are all socialized to regard people in prison as animals. I had been taught to feel that way. That's the way our society regards prisoners. Unless they actually do what I did and go in and meet the inmates."

Joe decided to go back South and went to Nashville, Tennessee. He, along with three others, started the Southern Coalition on Jails and Prisons in the spring of 1974 in six Southern states. Over the years it was expanded to eight states. In the beginning they were not even thinking about the death penalty for it had been struck down.

Joe is the director of the Southern Coalition on Jails and Prisons. Ordained in the United Church of Christ, his ministry is death row — the "congregation of the condemned" he calls it. Most of his time is spent with death row inmates and in comforting family members. He lobbies governors, congressmen, members of the press and whomever else it takes to get sentences commuted and to rid the judicial system of the death penalty.

"We got the whole organization involved in death row in the spring of nineteen seventy-six, as we felt that the Supreme Court was going to reinstate the death penalty. It got more intense as time went on. We've done everything from visiting governors to finding lawyers to trying to keep people alive no matter what it takes. There's been almost a hundred people executed since we started. We're just involved in a whole range of activities about the death penalty.

"When you sit and try to figure out why people support the death penalty, it all boils down to only one thing — revenge. I am a Christian and what can a Christian say? I can't be a vengeful person, and I can't make the state into the instrument of my revenge. The ability to think critically led me to reach this important conclusion in my life."

The Coalition, which has about 20 employees at offices in all of the Southern states, has been under the leadership of Pastor Ingle. They build opinion against the death penalty and give moral and financial support to individuals who have been sentenced to death. An important part of this work is finding attorneys to volunteer their services to those who cannot afford an attorney. Public legal assistance is terminated when a case has passed the lower court. Most death row inmates have had court-appointed attorneys.

There was a riot in 1975 in Tennessee's state prison. Joe Ingle was called in to negotiate on behalf of the prisoners. He and the prisoners negotiated with the administration all night long. "Once again the prisoners operated in good faith," Joe says, "and we worked out a compromise with the administration. But while we were doing so, they ordered in the cops and highway patrol and they came in and overpowered the inmates. They beat them, and put dogs on them. We didn't know what was going on for we were in the basement of the administration building and you are kind of sealed off there.

"The next morning when I found out what had happened, I went to the prison hospital. I'll never forget this one kid, his parents had come down from East Tennessee when they had heard he was seriously injured. He was sitting up in his bed. He had been literally beaten black and blue. Someone had taken a billy club and just clobbered this kid. We filed suit for the people who had been hurt by the police. We won a few thousand dollars for six different people.

"We also filed a statewide condition suit and that led to what we know now as the Grubb suit. In nineteen eighty the judge said the whole prison was unconstitutional. Since then the state has been forced to comply with the court orders in terms of how many inmates you can have in the prison system, and if you can double cell them."

Since then there has been some progress. Tennessee has single cells in the main prison now. In 1975 when the suit was started they had people packed in worse than sardines. Tennessee had one of the highest murder rates of any prison in the United States. Today that is not true. It's the result of the lessening of overcrowding.

"After an inmate has been sentenced to die, his appeals automatically start. They go through the state courts and then to the Supreme Court. This whole process takes from eight to twelve years to finish and unless someone drops their appeal, they will not die immediately.

"In nineteen eighty-four Ron Harries dropped his appeals and Bill Groseclose, another death row inmate and a friend, when into court and said that Harries wasn't competent to make that decision. He wasn't competent for several reasons. The coalition felt that the conditions on death row had really affected his judgment, and we alleged and then proved that Ron Harries had suffered extreme impairments over the years. He had a history of being institutionalized. It's really sad. We got all the documents, and Judge Nixon ruled that Harries was not competent.

"As a result of that, the momentum of executions in Tennessee has been slowed. The judge will have to rule on the condition suit, and unless someone drops his appeals I don't think we will have executions in this state this year [1989] and probably not next year either. People are being executed left and right in other states. We are very lucky here to have been able to put the brakes on that process through the courts.

"I've got little doubt that Jesus Christ would not have sat still for executions. Jesus said that if you are my disciples, you respond with love, with forgiveness and reconciliation. Jesus knew that you don't stop murder by becoming a murderer. You stop the process by refusing to murder."

When asked if he was ever sorry that he had chosen this life rather than a community church, Joe's reply is quick. "My church is the folks on death row—the congregation of the condemned. I am sorry, not about not having a nice little church, but I feel like Isaiah did. 'How long, O Lord, how long?' How many people are we going to kill? How long will this madness go on? When I sit there with someone's child weeping and trying to understand why daddy is being exterminated by the state, I wonder, My God, how long?"

Over the years Joe has visited all the death rows in the South. He has corresponded with over 400 of the 1200 persons sentenced to die. He has become friends with those who do not have relatives or whose families do not want to have contact with them. He is with the inmates at the last. Because of his efforts many sentences have been commuted to life imprisonment.

"I feel that I am called to do this type of work. I feel like this is what the Lord wants me to do. I do not go into a prison and lay a guilt trip on someone for not being a Christian. It's been my experience that the way you relate to an inmate is the way you relate to anyone else. When you are nice to them, they will return the respect. That's the way I operate. As a result I've got a lot of good friends on death row. Unfortunately eighteen of them have been killed by the state.

"That's been hard to deal with, to get close to someone and then they get killed no matter how hard you work for them. I'm able to maintain a balance because I can come home to Tennessee into a situation where we don't have an immediate threat of an execution. Now, if I had to go to Florida and all the other states for an execution and then come home to one, I'd probably be ready for a looney bin."

Joe is married and recently adopted a baby girl. They live on a 22-acre farm just outside of Ashland City highway. When asked if this job interferes with his personal life, Joe replies, "I guess it does. Willie Darden is a good example. He was executed last month. People have committed murder since Cain and Abel. Just because someone commits the act doesn't mean they are nonhuman. They're still a child of God, just like you and me. Willie had asked me to be at his execution, but since he heard we had just adopted a little girl he told me to stay home with my family. But I've known him since nineteen seventy-seven and there was no way I could not go down. I didn't want to be in that hellhole in Florida State Prison but the fact of the matter is I needed to be there for Willie and me. Sure it interferes with your personal life but my wife Becca and I talk about that and really deal with it.

"I don't know when we will stop murdering people, whether randomly on the streets or systematically in our death chambers. The only way to prevent continuation of the suffering and grief murder occasions is to prevent murder. I don't know how to stop the twenty thousand murders we inflict on each other a year. However, I do know that we can prevent additional grief and pain to the families of the condemned by simply halting executions. Murder has enough victims in our society without the state creating a whole new class of murder victims' families — the families of the executed."

Joe Ingle is a firm believer in alternative sentencing. "We have people in prison that do not belong there. In Tennessee sixty-one percent of the people in prison are in for nonviolent crimes. We ought to have them in restitution programs where they are paying back the people they committed the crimes on. Even more we need for the victim and the perpetrator to sit down and work out a restitution. If the courts did that instead of paying eighteen thousand dollars a year to lock him up, they'd be doing the taxpayers a favor. The chances of that person committing another crime are virtually nil once they know the person they've committed the crime against. It's a whole lot cheaper to do that. We would like to see some alternatives to incarceration in this state.

"On death row I think the solution is to have a mandatory twenty year sentence for anyone committing first degree murder. Then they are up for parole. That's our substitute for the death penalty. Because our belief is if someone is innocent when they are executed they are gone. You can't say 'I'm sorry.' That person's family is grieving and that person is dead. But if you have someone serving time you can always rectify that mistake. If you can prove that they are innocent, you can get them back in society. If they are dead you can't do that. We stress life as an alternative."

The Georgia office was just successful in getting an amendment to the death penalty that says you cannot execute the retarded. This has been a long struggle starting back in 1985. That will help to set a precedent for Tennessee, for Georgia is not a liberal state. It has executed more people than any other state in the United States.

Last year the coalition was successful in not allowing juveniles to be executed for their crimes. In Tennessee we had that written in the law in 1980 so that is not a possibility here. "I think what is most important to me is the personal relationships with some of the death row inmates. When you get to know someone on death row and care about them, you will do anything you can to stop the execution. They are friends just like on the outside."

Medical care for inmates is another major concern of Joe Ingle. "Medical care for those on death row is just not there. One example is James Adams, a death row inmate in Florida whom I knew for years. He was a rock man, which means he worked on the walkway cleaning. The guards put Drano in his food. He got violently sick and they had to take him to the hospital and treat him. It's a sad comment that the state of Florida was able to get away with that. Frankly, we were trying so hard to keep James alive that we didn't get a chance to file charges as soon as we could. To think of guards actually doing that just lets you know that to talk about medical care in a prison is like a joke. In Louisiana the doctors say that the guys are on death row, why do they need care? How do you deal with an attitude like that?

"I think this work has destroyed a lot of people. I know some who have had breakdowns just having to deal with the onslaught of executions. When you see what happens to the families of the condemned it's enough to make you cry, and I do. I was with Willie Darden's wife right after he was executed. What can you say? You can just be there and hold her and let her know that someone cares about her, that the good Lord loves her and you hope that somehow she feels the strength to maintain. There's a lot of heartbreaking work in all of this.

"We have studies to show that executing a person is more expensive than keeping him in prison. Who are we to put a price on a man's life? To say to you that your life is worth a hundred thousand dollars but not a hundred and five thousand is ridiculous. Human life is sacred and we should be protecting it. We shouldn't be talking about how much it costs to exterminate somebody.

A 1982 study in New York, for example, calculated the cost of reinstating the death penalty there and concluded that the average capital trial and first stage of appeals would cost the taxpayer about $1.8 million. That's more than twice what it cost to keep a person in prison for life. A capital trial normally takes much longer than one in which the death penalty is not involved, and lengthy appeals follow. Trial and appeal costs, including the time of judges, prosecutors, public defenders and court reporters, and the high costs of briefs are all borne by the taxpayers. *Time* magazine reported that the commutation of the death

sentences of 15 Arkansas prisoners saved the state an estima
million, considering the many appeals that would have been ar

For those who quote the Bible in saying they believe in the d
sentences Joe has a ready answer. "In the Old Testament there are
twenty-six references for the death penalty, but you look in the New
Testament and there isn't even one. There is no indication in Matthew,
Mark, Luke or John that Jesus would be interested in killing anybody.
No one is going to tell me that in nineteen eighty-nine anyone is going
to advocate executing people for talking back to their parents, or for
adultery, which they did in the Old Testament. And if you advocate that
you're a Christian and are for the death penalty, basically you are saying
that you believe Jesus tolerates the death penalty. If you look in the
eighth chapter of John not only did he speak out against the killing of
one woman, but he raised the whole question of us judging people.
When Christ was executed, he said about his enemies with his dying
words: 'Father, forgive them.'

"When I talk to someone who is for the death penalty I try to find
out where they are coming from. People have all different feelings about
it. I try to find out why they are for it. They are usually for it because
they feel it is a deterrent, and there is no information to support that.
In *The Case Against the Death Penalty* it says about deterrence:

> Persons who commit murders do not expect to get caught so the threat
> of dying in the electric chair has no deterrent effect on them. The vast ma-
> jority of capital crimes is committed during moments of great emotional
> stress, in fear, or under the influence of drugs or alcohol. In the cases
> where the crime is premeditated, the criminal expects to escape detection.
> Evidence shows that the death penalty is no more effective than imprison-
> ment in deterring crime. Where the death penalty is used there is no
> decrease in the rate of criminal homicide. In Philadelphia, there were as
> many murders after well-publicized executions as before. Death penalty
> states as a group do not have lower rates of criminal homicide than non-
> death-penalty states. States that abolish the death penalty do not show
> an increased rate of criminal homicide after abolition. In addition, cases
> have been clinically documented where the death penalty actually incited
> the capital crimes that it was supposed to deter. After reviewing studies
> in 1976, the United States Supreme Court found no conclusive evidence
> that the death penalty deters violent crime. The United Nations came to
> a similar conclusion.

"I think the only honest response to anyone who says they are for
the death penalty is to help them to see that what they are out for is
revenge. That's the only legitimate reason for the death penalty. I feel
that if you are a Christian and go around talking about revenge you have
a problem.

"I can understand revenge though. If you lose someone in your family and you want the person who committed the murder killed, at least that's an honest feeling. A clear indication of revenge is a woman here in town named Anna LeVin-Aaron. Her husband was murdered, Andy Barefoot was arrested and executed for this crime. I told Anna that I do not believe the killing of Barefoot has accomplished anything beyond creating more suffering and grief. In this case, the mourners are the Barefoot family. Anna said when he was executed that finally she could finish grieving. She had felt that as long as Andy lived it was as if her husband's life wasn't important.

"I knew Andy's sister, Susan Barefoot. She was upset when her brother was about to be killed. She wept, she hurt, and she felt all the despair and grief Anna had expressed. As she sat crying, she said to me, 'Joe, I'm a victim. My family is a victim too. When will it ever stop?' There is enough pain from murder in this society without the state sanctioning it and creating even more pain for people like Susan Barefoot. Surely, society does not want to perpetuate the suffering of Anna by transfering it to Susan."

Joe feels that one day we will look upon the death penalty as we now look upon the burning of witches. It's just a matter of time before people in this country realize that this is barbaric and is something that must be stopped.

In the *USA Death Penalty Briefing,* it talks about the arbitrariness of death sentencing:

> Killer lives, accomplice executed. In one case there was doubtful evidence of intent on the part of the executed prisoner that a killing should occur. In the other the actual killer received a lesser sentence owing to chance circumstances.
>
> Texas prisoner Doyle Skillern and an accomplice were both found guilty of the 1974 murder of an undercover police agent. The accomplice fired six shots into the victim and was sentenced to life imprisonment. Doyle Skillern, who had been sitting in a nearby car, was sentenced to death and was executed in January 1985 — just before the accomplice became eligible for parole.
>
> Roosevelt Green is reported to have been somewhere else when the killing in his case occurred. He had gone for gas when a co-defendant raped and murdered the victim. The trial judge said that Roosevelt was only an accomplice in a murder committed by another person and his participation in the homicidal act was relatively minor. However the Georgia Supreme Court upheld his conviction saying that he should not have left the victim alone with a man he knew to be dangerous. He was executed in March 1985.

As a result of Joe's efforts, several prisoners have had sentences commuted. In March, 1987, one man, Joseph Green Brown, was released after 14 years on death row in Florida. He had been within 15 hours of being executed on one occasion. The Southern Coalition has assisted in proving that Joseph Brown was innocent.

"People do not understand that execution is a painful form of death. The law is written in each state that the person is to be conscious of what is going on. He understands that he is being killed. That's why the Supreme Court ruled that they could not kill the insane. Because they did not know they were being killed. It's hard to believe what happened in the case of Louie Fransis in Louisiana. They strapped him in the electric chair and ran the electricity through him. It didn't kill him, the chair malfunctioned. They pulled him out and his attorney said, 'You cannot put him back in that chair, it's cruel and unusual punishment.' It went all the way to the Supreme Court and they said that he could be executed. Sure enough, they took Louie and put him back in the chair and killed him. That's how barbaric this thing is."

Amnesty International says in *USA Death Penalty Briefing* that it is inhumane to execute inmates.

> In a 1983 electrocution in Alabama, it took three charges of 1,000 volts over a period of 14 minutes to kill the prisoner. After the second charge smoke and flame erupted from his left temple.
> In a 1984 electrocution, witnesses saw the condemned prisoner struggle to breathe for eight minutes after the first two-minute charge of electricity had failed to kill him.
> In another execution by lethal gas in Mississippi, the prisoner is reported to have had convulsions for eight minutes and to have struck his head repeatedly on the pole behind him. Some witnesses claimed that he was not yet dead when deputies asked them to leave the witness room.
> In yet another execution by lethal injection in Texas, the prisoner took at least ten minutes to die. A year later technicians in Texas were reported to have spent 40 minutes searching a condemned prisoner's limbs for a suitable vein in which to insert the needle.

"I think we just have to remember that we will live to see the end of the death penalty in this country. It's just a firm conviction that I have. Basically, I don't think the good Lord is going to sit still for this. We've got to educate the American people about the death penalty. They do not understand how it's working. They do not understand that nine out of ten people on death row had court-appointed lawyers because they are all poor."

A defendant's poverty, lack of firm social roots in the community, inadequate legal representation at trial or on appeal—all are common factors among death row populations. Clinton Duffy, longtime warden of San Quentin, and witness to over 150 executions, has testified that in his experience capital punishment is "a privilege of the poor." Justice William O. Douglas noted in the *Furman* decision,* "One searches in vain for the execution of any member of the affluent strata of this society."

There is evidence that many defendants are assigned inexperienced counsel who are ill-equipped to handle such cases. A recent study found that capital defendants in Texas with court-appointed attorneys were more than twice as likely to receive a death sentence than those with retained counsel.

"They do not understand that another thing that sends you to death row is the race of the victim. If you are convicted of killing a white person you are a whole lot more likely to get the death sentence than if you killed a black person.

"Different parts of states give the death penalty more often than other parts. A study of criminal homicide cases in Georgia found that just fifteen percent of Georgia's hundred and fifty-nine counties were responsible for eighty-five percent of death sentences imposed in the state from nineteen seventy-three to nineteen seventy-eight. It also found that death sentences were six times more likely to be imposed in the more rural central region of Georgia than in the north, and seven to eight times more likely than in Fulton County. A U.S. Department of Justice report on capital punishment noted that nearly sixty-three percent of those under the sentence of death in nineteen eighty-four were held by states in the South.

"I have worked with eighteen people who have been executed and five of those I'm convinced were innocent. Willie Darden, Tim Baldwin in Louisiana, James Adams, Bob Sullivan and Edward Johnson. There are people who are innocent who get the death penalty. It happens all the time."

In the Bedau and Radelet report on the "Miscarriages of Justice in Potentially Capital Cases," it was reported that nine individuals under sentences of death imposed in the last 15 years were released in the first six months of 1987 because of evidence raising doubts about their guilt. We now know of 24 defendants sentenced to death since the *Furman* decision, of whom 23 were later freed because of doubts about their guilt and one executed despite such doubts.

In Florida, two black men, Freddie Pitts and Wilbert Lee, were released from prison after 12 years awaiting execution for a murder they

---

*The *Furman* decision: The Supreme Court in 1972 held that arbitrary and capricious application of the death penalty violated the Eighth Amendment against cruel and unusual punishment.

never committed. Had the execution taken place, two more innocent men would have died.

In 1984 Earl Charles won a suit for damages against a Savannah, Georgia, police officer for framing him on a murder charge. After nearly four years on death row, he was released when the district attorney's own reinvestigation of the case convinced him that Charles was innocent.

Two

Mary Kaki Friskics-Warren

Kaki Friskics-Warren went to the Texas University when she first became interested in working with the prisoners. One of her professors worked with inmates. She became involved with him at FCI of Fort Worth, Texas. After two years she went to Nashville, Tennessee, and studied to become a minister at Vanderbilt.

"Jeff Blum and I started the Reconciliation House Ministry in nineteen eight-four," she says. She wanted to work with the inmates on death row. During the old administration she and Jeff Blum were allowed to go on the row and talk to the men there. They would counsel the inmates and get personal things for them such as cards for birthdays, Mother's Day and other holidays. They also would go and talk to the men where something had happened in the family such as a death or illness. They were the ones who would bring the news and give comfort to them. Then with the new administration all that changed. They were not allowed on the row anymore. They could visit an inmate but would have to be on that person's visitation list. Since this was not helping the men, they decided to work with the family members and Reconciliation House was born.

Reconciliation House is a large house that was used to serve the families and friends of inmates in Tennessee. The house will accommodate up to twenty visitors at one time. All guests enjoy sleeping accommodations, bath facilities, a stocked kitchen, lounge with television, and transportation to and from the prison to visit. "By offering a warm welcome and helpful support, we hope to encourage visitation to those who are imprisoned." There is no charge for this service, and it is given to allow families to visit their loved one in prison who may not otherwise be able to afford the visits.

"In addition to the Guest House, we visit in the prison of Tennessee

12

and advocate for prisoners. We recruit volunteers to visit one on one with prisoners. We also educate the community and churches about prisons and the criminal justice system and train ministers how to deal with members of their churches who are victims or perpetrators of crime.

"The group Separate Prisons was started in October of nineteen eighty-five by Zel Morris, Shirley Vanarsdale, Cheryal Smith and myself. We started meeting in the office with just a few family members and from there we grew slowly. We are a support group of women who have a loved one in prison. They can talk to each other about things with which they are all familiar. They voice their fears, hopes and offer comfort to each other in times of trials and heartbreak. They support each other like one big happy family. They are not shunned by each other like outsiders sometimes do once they find out you have someone in prison and especially on death row.

"We are a unit, bonded in spirit, with the knowledge that we are all in the same boat so they know how each other feels. Sometimes we have a speaker come and talk to the women about the problems that occur at the prison. If someone in the group is going through a bad time, the others are there to help them through it all. Our group has been growing and new groups are forming in Memphis and Kingsport, Tennessee."

Reconciliation was recently honored to receive second place in the Hospital Corporation of America's 1987 Awards in Nonprofit Management. They also had the prison telephone rates reduced. An inmate can only call collect. Local calls were $1.25 and they have now been reduced to 75¢ per call.

"No one needs to tell you about the hardships a family faces when they have a loved one in prison. The pains of separation, isolation, fear and anger are real. Families must struggle to stay together through the time of incarceration and sometimes families can use some help. There are numerous opportunities and places for your family to receive the help they need.

"We have a Wilderness program for the children. We take them camping once a year. They experience sleeping under lean-tos, cooking over an open fire, hiking, rock climbing, and even cave exploring. Over a campfire the children talk about the events of the day, read, and for the first time maybe talk about having a parent in prison. Most of the kids can't talk about their parent at school or to friends as the others just don't understand what it means to have a parent in prison. In the campfire's light we saw a connection between being in prison and rock climbing. Our loved ones in prison often feel like they can't take the next step. They need family to be there saying, 'I love you! I believe in you. And I'll help you through this.'

"Can the success of such an experience be measured? Probably not. How could we begin to measure fears confronted, self-confidence gained, community built? The Wilderness Camping Experience was a special event for each person who participated and we know now we must do it again next year.

"I'd like to see the death penalty abolished and also see some proportionate sentencing. I'd like to see all families be able to visit the picnic area. I feel that there is a need for prisons but they need to treat people as humans.

"As a faithful person I eventually see the death penalty being abolished. As a practical one I don't see it in our lifetime. What the public can do to assist us is to open their minds to the concept that the families are victims. We could also use money as we are run on strictly donations. The address is Reconciliation, P.O. Box 90827, Nashville, Tennessee 37209.

"My job is stressful but it also has a lot of happy times too. The most difficult is telling someone in prison that a family member is dead. Nothing can be more devastating than being locked up in prison when a loved one dies. You cannot even attend the funeral. A lot of times my family life has been put on hold. I work sometimes sixteen hours a day for there is just so much to do. The other side has been the good things that have happened. Weddings and babies being born. I get to share in the most intimate part of people's lives."

Three

Harmon Wray

Harmon Wray works part time with Project Return and teaches prison ministry at Vanderbilt Divinity School. He is also a volunteer coordinator for the Death Penalty Resistance Project of Tennessee.

"I guess I started getting involved in death penalty work in nineteen seventy-five. In nineteen seventy-six the Supreme Court decided in the ruling of death penalty statutes in three other Southern states, there was a way you could do the death penalty that was not unconstitutional, even though four years before that, it was discriminatory and unfair. It began to look like other states were going to write laws that were very much like the ones the Court had upheld in nineteen seventy-six.

"We could see this coming and John Lozier, who is a staff person for Southern Prison Ministry, decided to start a statewide anti–death penalty organization in Tennessee to begin to ward off this plan that was coming up in nineteen seventy-seven. I was one of the people who was involved in the initial meeting that we held in October of nineteen seventy-six. Out of that we began an organization called Tennesseans Against the Death Penalty.

"We were able to put together a public hearing of the two judiciary committees of the two houses in the Legislature. We had some thirty witnesses testify and read statements opposed to the introduction of the death penalty in Tennessee again. They ended up voting to pass the bill out onto the floor. When it was voted on by the whole Legislature, it passed. Governor Ray Blanton vetoed that bill; he was opposed to the death penalty and campaigned against it. It was passed even over his veto and became law."

It was at that time that people began to get the death sentence and Tennessee's death row began to fill up. "A lot of my early work involved going around and talking to the churches trying to get them to contact

15

their legislators to vote against the death penalty. Probably the second person to come on death row after this law passed was Bill Groseclose. John Lozier began setting up a visitation program to match up people from the outside to visit people on the inside. Billy and I were matched up by him and for ten years we have been friends. We get together ever week or two to visit."

Tennesseans Against the Death Penalty has recently changed names. The are now the Death Penalty Resistance Project of Tennessee. They are just now getting started and will be putting together a steering committee and doing some fund raising. They put out a quarterly newsletter. There are about 800 people on the mailing list now, mostly in Tennessee. They have monthly meetings and spend a lot of time just trying to do legal and technical things. They also do a lot of community education, media talk shows, speaking gigs for church groups, classrooms, civic clubs or anyone who wants to hear them speak.

"The first thing I would like to see done to improve the whole system is to quit sending so many there. We are sending more people than we need to. Sometimes, because they are so overcrowded, we are letting out people before they are ready to get out. Mostly we are not giving them support when they are released. If we sent fewer people to prison in the first place, we could keep the ones in who are dangerous and need to be there. We would have more resources to help people when they came out and get them back on their feet. We would be able to do a lot more with them in the community, especially those who are first offenders, and help them get counseling and get jobs, whatever they need. We would make the inmate make restitution for the crime, which would be better for the criminals for they would be held accountable for what they did.

"It would be better for the taxpayers because restitution programs and alcohol programs, even though they cost money, don't cost near as much money as prisons do. I believe that we should just stop building prisons, close down some of the ones we have, and use the other ones better. We need to upgrade them, have more drug and alcohol counseling and educational programs for the people who are locked up. Just ask ourselves what is it we are trying to accomplish. The more people we lock up, the longer we keep them locked up, the worse we treat them, the more damaged they're going to be when they get out. Therefore, they will be more dangerous to us.

"The public needs to wake up and look critically at the issues and don't believe the politicians. Anybody that can donate their time and money to the Death Penalty Resistance Project would be most appreciated. We need people to volunteer to help in this work. The other thing people can do is to contact public officials about the death sentence."

In the next two years the men on death row will be at the end of their appeals and we will start having executions here in Tennessee. The only thing that will stand between them and the electric chair is the governor. Governor Ned McWherter has said, "I think capital punishment ought to be implemented. That ought to be at the top of the list of priorities." He won't have any problems in executing inmates.

"The killings will be carried out with our tax money, by our elected and appointed officials, and ostensibly to protect and avenge us, the citizens of Tennessee," Harmon says. "As criminal defense attorneys pursue, hopefully with success in individual cases, the legal issues regarding the use of capital punishment, it is up to the rest of us to do what we can do to educate the media, the public, and the politicians about a number of things: the uselessness of the death penalty, the true meaning and value of executive clemency as one part of the law which the governor is sworn to uphold, and the circumstances of particular cases which cry out for the positive use of clemency.

"In short, we need to be making it politically feasible and morally imperative for Governor McWherter to take a stand for mercy by commuting at least some death sentences to life in prison after legal appeals are exhausted. He needs to hear from as many of us as possible, as often as possible, beginning as soon as possible, that we do not want him to make killers of us all.

"The other people who need to be contacted by the public are their legislators. Probably in 1990 there's going to be a bill that will change the form of execution from the electric chair to lethal injections. This was tried in Tennessee a few years ago and was defeated in the Legislature. Our belief is, if that law were passed, it would simply be a way to let people off the hook, to make it more acceptable to the public, make it seem as if they were not really killing anybody. Kind of like putting a dog to sleep. We oppose that very strongly and we're hoping that people will defeat the bill again. There's no humane way to kill people.

"We were able to get a bill passed a few years ago that increased the amount of money that lawyers could be paid by the state for indigent clients. We've lately been trying to get established a capital punishment resource center which would help to upgrade the quality of legal defense that people get on capital cases."

Harmon says that one of the things they are working on now is to make sure the new facilities being built continue to have contact visits for the men on death row. Tennessee has had that all along (contrary to most other states) and has no problem with it. Inmates who are allowed to have contact visits tend to be happier and thus do not get into as much trouble. Contact with family members is necessary to have the inmate survive in the kind of atmosphere they are forced to live in.

"I think the death penalty is stupid, horrible, and immoral, sinful and criminal. I'm against it because of my Christian faith. I believe it's completely contrary to the Gospel. Under no circumstances should anyone be executed for any reason by any government. I don't think the state has the right to do that. It has the power, but not the right. Christians ought to be doing everything they can to see that the state does not have the power to execute. The people have the power to change things."

Harmon feels that its hard to separate his personal life from the work. It's very personal to him, and he cannot just forget about the death penalty once he's off work. His work is not a paying job but he takes it very seriously, spending many hours a week fighting the death sentence.

"The conditions on death row haven't changed much since it was ruled unconstitutional. They went on a level system for the inmates with different programs depending on what level they are on. I think there is too much power on the part of some of the people who work on death row. They use their prejudice against death row prisoners to make sure they are at lower levels. That means they get fewer privileges. The higher numbers get to go out of their cells more, they get to do a lot more activities, and have something meaningful to spend their time on.

The Death Penalty Resistance Project's address is P.O. Box 120552, Nashville, Tennessee 37212. The phone number is 615-256-7028. Write to Harmon Wray or Kathryn Hearne.

Four

Jeff Blum

Jeff began working with juveniles when he was still in college. He had read about the mass executions of the Jews in Germany. When he got to the Divinity School, he started visiting the inmates here in Tennessee on death row.

"I realized that a lot of the guys I came in contact with on death row were like some of the juveniles I had dealt with. They did not have the proper resources or people helping them out. I felt the United States was doing the same thing as Germany did to the Jews only on a smaller scale. Whenever you take human life that way, when the state systematically kills someone, it demeans all of us. It's not only bad for the person being killed, but for all of us. It makes us all more barbaric. That's why I started getting involved.

"I worked for six years with the Southern Prison Ministry visiting the inmates and providing Mother's Day cards or whatever the guys needed at that point. The system did not provide attorneys at the appellate level. I started recruiting attorneys to take on cases for the guys who needed them. We started providing resources for the attorneys to use whether they were actually trying cases or on the appeals. When the Southern Prison Ministry started changing its focus there was not strong support for the work that was being done for those on death row. I eventually left Southern Prison Ministry and took a part time position at a criminal defense lawyer's association. We developed a couple of death penalty manuals and it's been good to work for them.

"They are not as a group against capital punishment as I would like them to be, but they are willing to be supportive to certain elements of anti–death penalty work like making sure people have attorneys and doing things in the Legislature that make the application of the death penalty, while it never is fair, at least somewhat fairer than it now is."

19

They have a manual for death penalty rules, and provide resources to attorneys at trial level. They have a statewide membership of attorneys so most of them know there are resources available when a lawyer gets a death penalty case. They call, and are sent a manual. If an attorney needs some sort of expert during a trial, such as forensic, they provide that service to them. They give seminars to help attorneys pick juries, get through sentencing phases, investigations. These men are trained at the seminar to do this type of work.

"At the point where a person is convicted and goes through the direct appeal process, and no longer has an attorney, we make sure one is available to them. There is a separate thing we are involved in right now, that in the long range we hope will have some positive effect. A commission was established to study what is going on legally on capital punishment. On this commission was the attorney general and judges, defense attorney and Supreme Court justices, people who were not anti-death penalty, but were worried about how much money they would need to do death penalty work.

"Some commission members were able to achieve a recommendation that we needed a full time death penalty resource center. This would have three attorneys, and two staff people available to attorneys at all levels of the process to write briefs to develop resources specific to death penalty cases in Tennessee, to go over briefs to make sure they were properly done, to do investigations into jury patterns, to make sure the juries that are sitting on these cases are proper. This center has been developed and we have a commitment from the Federal Government for a hundred and sixty thousand dollars to set it up.

"It's an interesting sort of process because we are getting support from people on the other side of the issue. For them it's a basic fairness issue. The realization that even if you're for the death penalty, just because of the nature of the punishment, you want to make sure it's a fair process. For us setting up this resource center is an important step in fighting the death penalty.

"I think the worst problem on death row is how bad things are getting. If you are going to have a death row, I would think it would be very important that there be some increase in contact with free world people. One of the things I've been fighting for for years now is increased contact for people like myself who are trying to monitor where the inmates' cases are in the legal system. Some of the cases fall through the cracks if we don't have a constant reading of where they are. Constant interaction with the inmates to find out where they are is what we need.

"I think jobs are real important to the guys that are down there, and education programs. I don't think they should be on death row. If they are condemned, they should live where the rest of the inmates are housed. They should be allowed to do things that the general prison population can do. Since nineteen seventy-seven we have fifteen guys on death row who have had their sentences overturned and are serving a life sentence. Why not just keep them in the population until they are close to being executed and then put them in segregation. All the other inmates who have committed murder and not gotten the death sentence are out there. It's the town where the inmate was sentenced that determines what sentence he receives. One murderer will get twenty years, and another will get the death sentence.

Jeff believes that, some time, the death sentence will be overturned. It's such an absurd type of punishment that it will be outlawed. In the meantime we have to have structures that make it just as difficult as possible for people to execute people.

"I think the people need to be aware of what is going on in the Legislature. Narrowing the scope of capital punishment needs to be supported. Right now we are considering a move to make it illegal to execute retarded people. Some states have already done that and others have made a move to do it.

"I think in Tennessee Micky Matson is a prime target of that. Someone who is retarded enough that in other states, he would not be executed. Criminal defense lawyers are burdened with a responsibility to insure fairness in our society. Everyone, regardless of how terrible the crime they are accused of doing — the attorney has to go into that situation believing that person is innocent. The bottom line is unless it's done properly, the person should be found innocent.

"We are constantly trying to improve the quality of representation that a client gets. That is the most important thing that we are about. You can't ever give up, the laws are always changing and it's a constant struggle to keep up.

"Prison Condition lawsuits never accomplish what they set out to do. That is to improve the overall conditions the inmates are living in. Overall, I think the conditions are worse now than before the lawsuit was filed making the death penalty unconstitutional. Even if you had everything perfect and the guards were mad at you for one reason or another, then they are going to make it miserable for the inmates. You see situations where a guard will goad the inmate to acting out in such a way as to have his level moved to a four. This is the lowest level and one with the least privileges. Then the person is put in the worst possible environment.

"In the beginning I thought the media coverage was the way to go. I would try to humanize death row clients but what has happened is that the other side has learned to use the media. In any given situation the victim of the murder will always look better than the person that committed that murder. No matter how retarded, or poor, or innocent. Even if they are innocent the victim always looks better than this person. So the press does us a great deal of disservice.

"My present dealing with the media is: the less said the better; the less a particular person is in the media, the better. When someone like Ron Harries gets into the media, it brings out the victim's family full force and they really start coming at you. Once again, public sentiment is such that we can't win on a one to one vote. We have to win at getting these cases in the court and making sure they are litigated properly. We have not said anything to the press about getting this resource center started. We have the support of people and as long as it doesn't come out that they are supporting us, they're going to be supportive, but if someone were to go the press with this and suddenly they are asked, it would become a death penalty issue. Then we might lose."

Five

Watt Espy

For the past 18 years, Watt Espy has documented 15,940 cases of legal executions in the United States. "It started purely as a hobby. I have always been sort of a crime buff," he replied when asked what motivated him to start this research. "I found so many inaccuracies in various journalistic writings about executions. I set out not only to chronicle and document as many executions as possible, but wanted to get all the facts of each case."

Watt lives in one half of a large grey house near the edge of downtown Headland, Alabama. Inside the house he has over two hundred pictures of those who have been executed hanging on his walls. He lives surrounded by death every time an inmate dies on death row. He was born and raised in Headland. Before he began his research, he earned a living as a salesman.

Watt's grandfather founded Headland National Bank; his father was president and chief executive officer for several years. His brother Mark holds the title today.

"I have run across plenty of those who were innocent of the crime for which they were convicted and executed. I have found cases where people were executed for murder and their alleged victims turned up alive. Obviously, they were innocent of the crime for which they were executed. The death penalty is bound to be applied to innocent people no matter what our safeguards against such mistakes are.

"I concede that most of the people who have been executed in this country have been guilty of the crimes for which they were convicted. However, there also have been plenty of innocent people, subsequently proven innocent beyond a shadow of a doubt, to have been deprived of their lives by due process of law. In addition to those proven innocent after their execution there are others, I am sure, who were innocent but

23

have never been proven to be so, because law enforcement officials and prosecutors will not investigate a case once an execution has been held. The case is closed for them, and it is probably too much to expect them to go out and try to prove that they have executed an innocent person no matter what the evidence.

"To my way of thinking nothing can be more horrible or repugnant than that the state, with all its power for good or evil, should deprive one of its citizens of life for a crime committed by another. I cannot imagine any human being, who is not a perfect monster himself, viewing with unconcern the prospect of an innocent man being executed, but that possibility always exists where the death penalty is available.

"James Adams, a black man, was sentenced to die by an all white jury in Florida for a felony murder of a white man. All through the appeals, he maintained he was innocent. One witness testified that the person he saw leaving the victim's house was definitely not Adams. The forensic evidence that was gathered strongly suggested that he was not the perpetrator. That evidence was withheld until after the trial and sentencing. A recent investigation by a twenty-year veteran of the Philadelphia Police Department's Homicide Unit argues convincingly that Adams was innocent."

A recently released study on wrongful convictions, by Hugo Bedau and Michael Radelet, listed James Adams as one of the 23 innocent persons executed in this century.

"In the state of Alabama, out of seven hundred and thirty-eight executed, we have every reason to believe that ten were innocent. The great proponents of capital punishment will say that's not a bad record at all: we executed seven hundred and twenty-eight guilty people. One of the differences in our form of government and that of a totalitarian system is that we believe it is better that guilty people go free than an innocent one be executed.

"There is virtually no state in this country where you've had a number of executions, that didn't execute innocent people."

Rape is a charge that sent many innocent men to their death. Rape was primarily a Southern capital offense. Blacks were the primary target. In Alabama, no white man was ever executed for raping a black woman. If a black man was accused of being with a white woman, even if he had an ironclad alibi, many times the jury would still give him the death sentence. They would accuse the other blacks of lying to save their friend.

"Along with the innocent people being executed, we have to consider the execution of the insane. During the nightmare regime of Adolf Hitler, the Jews were not the only persons to be liquidated. The insane and those who suffered from various mental and physical disorders were shot, hanged, gassed and used for medical experiments. The civilized world recoiled in horror at this excessive use of death as an instrument of state policy. Yet insane persons have been executed in the United States. Where the man whose life is in jeopardy is penniless and friendless with no funds with which to employ adequate analysts to examine him and to testify for him, the only psychiatrists available have generally been those from state hospitals who, in all too many instances, have given only perfunctory examinations, frequently for as short a time as fifteen minutes in a cell of the accused and who, in practically every instance, have served as an extension of the prosecution arm of the state certifying a man to be sane enough to be executed.

"As long as the death penalty remains on the statutes there is always the possibility that people who are not responsible will be put to death by the state, which has an obligation to take care of them and to protect them from themselves and others. In so many cases the execution of the insane is the expedient and popular thing to do, but it is never the right thing to do. If the state can kill the retarded, then the state can close down its mental hospitals and set up a crematorium on the grounds, or a gas chamber, as Hitler did."

When Watt Espy first started out, he was undecided on capital punishment. "I don't even believe in hunting and fishing. I don't believe in killing or any kind of violence. Now that doesn't mean fighting for my country. I served in the Navy and if my country was threatened, I wouldn't mind bearing arms. But as far as violence and killing for the sake of killing, even animals and fish, I just don't believe in that.

"I tended to believe before I got into this work that there was a deterrent value to the death penalty. It only took six months after I'd been into it, to come to the belief that there is no deterrent value. Two wrongs don't make a right, it's just that simple. Those people who claim the death penalty is a deterrent have never studied it. They've never had the empirical data on which to base their assumptions, and this is the first time that an effort has been made to collect the data upon which accurate assumptions can be made."

What he found in his research disturbed him, especially the children who had been executed.

One of his saddest cases deals with Hannah Ocuish, a 12-year-old retarded Indian girl, who was hanged in New London, Connecticut, in 1786 after being convicted of murdering a 6-year-old girl whom she had beaten to death for a basket of strawberries.

During his years of research, Watt has sought to understand the victim of the execution and the events leading up to the crime. He also finds out if they had an appeal and the legal representation provided, whether or not the inmate had a court-appointed attorney or had the funds to hire counsel himself. Sometimes he even finds out what they had for a last meal and the last words uttered.

"There's a very good reason for doing all of this. Because it has never been done. Most of the people legally executed have been poor, illiterate and members of racial or ethnic minorities. There is absolutely no deterrent value in the death sentence," he says. "There was a case in 1880 in which a man was convicted of killing his wife and was hanged. Three or four years later, his son killed his wife and was hanged. There was no deterrence there. If it didn't deter in this case, who the hell would it deter?

"George Speed, a black man, was hanged at Fayetteville, Georgia, for the rape of a white girl. His half-brother, Clarke Edmondson, was among the witnesses. That very night another white girl was assaulted. Edmondson confessed his guilt and was taken from the jail and lynched in the same gallows from which his brother had been legally hanged nine days earlier."

"If there were a deterrent value in executions, whether they be public or private, one would expect those closest to, and most aware of, capital cases and their penalties to be deterred by them.

"George Swearingen, who, as the sheriff of Cumberland County, Maryland, had served as a hangman and was fully aware of the horrors of slow strangulation at the gallows, was convicted of murdering his own wife, and was later hanged from his own scaffold.

"*Newsweek* magazine devoted much of its October seventeenth, nineteen eighty-three issue to the case of James Autry, who had just narrowly missed execution by lethal injection for the murder of a convenience-store clerk and one other person over a six-pack of beer. The magazine gave an excellent insight into the sad, disturbed and deprived childhood of James and his younger brother, Robert, each of whom was possibly the only person who ever really loved or cared for the other.

"James Autry's luck finally ran out and he was executed at the Texas State Prison on March fourteenth, nineteen eighty-four. Three months later, the younger brother was arrested and charged with the mutilation murder of an invalid woman. He was subsequently declared insane and committed.

"There can be no doubt that the execution of an individual serves as a limited deterrence in that he or she will certainly never again transgress against any laws of society, capital or otherwise. However, when we consider that this particular sentence of the law has always been and probably always will be applied in a capricious and haphazard fashion, the fact that there is virtually no general deterrent value should become obvious. One person convicted of an offense may be sentenced to die and be executed, while his crime partner, equally as guilty, but more fortunate in the selection of a trial jury, may, though convicted, receive only a prison sentence. If the state doesn't respect the sanctity for human life it's unlikely anyone else will."

F.E. Zimring, in *Perspectives on Deterrence,* notes that in Michigan, a state without the death penalty, the homicide rate between 1940 and 1955 averaged 3.49 per 100,000 population; in Indiana, which retains the death penalty, the rate was 3.5. When Delaware, without the death penalty between 1958 and 1961, restored capital punishment, the annual average homicide rate increased by 3.7 persons per 100,000.

"Perhaps the most disturbing aspect of the death penalty is that it is discriminately applied. There has always been discrimination in the application of capital punishment, and as long as death penalty laws remain on the statutes there always will be. With but a few exceptions, members of minorities, the poor, the friendless, the uneducated and, if you will pardon the expression, the different, are the ones who pay with their lives for their crimes.

"The black man who killed the white man has always been more likely to pay with his life than the white man who has killed the black man. This has been universally true in every state in this Union, not just the South.

"Let me conclude my comments on the discriminatory nature of the death penalty by mentioning a recent case. We are all familiar with the case of Dan White, the former San Francisco policeman and city councilman, an accepted member of the establishment, who entered the San Francisco City Hall through a back window with a loaded revolver and shot Mayor George Moscone and Councilman Harvey Milk to death. White promptly surrendered himself to the police at the station where he had previously been employed, wept and pleaded insanity, claiming that he had not meant to kill but offering no reason for sneaking into the offices armed. He was convicted of manslaughter and received a seven-year sentence after entering a plea of insanity.

"The same week that he was convicted, in the same state of California, another killer — a drifter who had killed several people and drank their blood — also pleaded insanity but was convicted of first degree murder and sentenced to die. To my way of thinking, White's crime was one of premeditated murder if there ever has been one. Also, to my way of thinking, one who drinks human blood, believing himself to be some sort of vampire or Dracula, is obviously insane and not a fit candidate for the gas chamber."

Watt lectures, does some writing, and sometimes even sells his research findings to help pay for his work. He hopes that sometime in the future his project will be housed in some university's library.

"The death penalty is a throwback to a less enlightened era. It serves no useful purpose. It is not a deterrent to crime nor does it restore life to the victim. It is demoralizing to the population in general in that it shows a lack of regard for the sanctity of human life by the state itself. Finally, the possibility of error exists and I am certain that everyone will agree with me that nothing can be more terrible or more reprehensible than for the state to unjustly take a life.

"Someday the death penalty will be eradicated in the United States, and we will look back on it as a part of our Dark Ages just as we now look back on the hanging of witches at Salem as an abomination we can no longer tolerate. If mankind is to survive on this planet, we must learn to live together and be civilized. The death penalty is not civilized. Let its demise begin with us."

Six

Patricia Smith

Patricia Smith is the associate director of the Georgia Association of Retarded Citizens. She was clemency attorney for Jerome Bowden, a retarded black man executed in Georgia.

"I was basically involved in the case of Jerome Bowden who was executed in Georgia two years ago. He was mentally retarded and had an I.Q. of fifty-nine, which classifies him as mildly retarded.

"He was convicted on his one confession. There was no other shred of evidence on him at all and it was highly questionable if the so-called confession that he gave was actually his confession. It simply was written in a way that he was not capable of doing. It was very logical and laid out all kinds of details that he did not have the capacity to give and I doubt that he had the capacity to remember the kind of details in that confession."

The jury which heard his case was never informed of his mental capacity. His retardation clearly should have been an issue in the case.

"That confession was used and he was convicted and sentenced to die. He was executed by that confession alone. That probably illustrates as graphically as anything can that the mentally retarded people are at the mercy of the system. They are unable to exercise their constitutional rights, they simply do not have the capacity to exercise the right to remain silent, their right not to sign a confession, their right to have a lawyer, and they do not even know what those things mean.

"When someone says to them, 'Do you waive your right to have an attorney present?' They do not know what waive means. If you ask someone who is mentally retarded what waive means, you will find them, waving their hands. If you ask them what an attorney means, they haven't a clue to what that means. If you treat a mentally retarded person

29

nicely and tell him you will help him, that all he has to do is sign this paper, he will sign anything. The chances are very high that he will not be able to read what is written down and even if he can read some of the words, he cannot comprehend what they mean. So you have people totally at the mercy of any sheriff or policeman who, because of public pressure, is out to find somebody he can call the guilty person and get the public off his back.

"That's basically the problem we deal with, with retarded people. All the potential errors that can be made in executing the wrong person, if that person has a normal intelligence, is multiplied by a factor of a hundred when you are dealing with one who is mentally retarded.

"These people will probably say they did anything. One of the major features of mentally retarded people is that they don't want to be seen as mentally retarded. They've learned a variety of ways to conceal their retardation. One of the way they conceal it is to be completely reliant on all authority figures. If an authority figure comes along and says, 'You did this didn't you?' in the beginning they might say no, but after awhile their feelings will be that the person who is saying this to them is very unhappy, and they will say that they did it. Not because they did it, but because their motivation is to make the person in authority happy, so that person will be kind to them."

Less than two years after Bowden's execution, on March 7, 1988, the Georgia legislature passed a bill prohibiting the imposition of the death penalty on the mentally retarded. It is the first such bill in the country.

Seven

Richard Moran

Richard Moran is a professor of sociology at Mt. Holyoke College in South Hadley, Massachusetts. He has written on the financial cost of capital punishment. When most people argue that the death penalty costs too much, they are usually speaking about the human and social costs of the state's decision to take a life. People who have made a study of the matter say that the death penalty costs too much and mean it literally. For instance, it is much more expensive than life imprisonment. Here is the reason, according to Richard Moran.

"In nineteen seventy-two the Supreme Court in *Furman v. Georgia* held that 'arbitrary' and 'capricious' application of the death penalty violated the Eighth Amendment's prohibition against 'cruel and unusual punishment.' This meant that a defendant had to be prosecuted and convicted in a way that was extraordinarily rigorous and free of any kind of prejudice. Since then the Supreme Court has fashioned what is generally called a super due process model for the death penalty cases.

"In a recent University of California at Davis *Law Review* article, Margot Garey has calculated that it costs a minimum of five hundred thousand dollars to complete a death penalty trial in California. And between August nineteen seventy-seven (when the current law took effect) and December nineteen eighty-five, only ten percent have actually resulted in a death sentence.

"We think it is fair to say that it costs the citizens of California about four and a half million dollars to sentence one person to death. Data from New York state suggest that if it adopted the death penalty the cost would be one million, eight hundred twenty-eight thousand, one hundred dollars per capital trial. Assuming even a seventy-five percent failure-rate, it would cost about seven point three million dollars to sentence one person to death in New York."

Not all people sentenced to death will be executed. Many if not most will have their sentences commuted to life imprisonment. "Even if we do not include the costs of keeping a man on death row for an average of four years prior to his execution (about one hundred sixty thousand dollars), or the cost to maintain and operate the gas chamber or the electric chair, and if we naively assume that all people condemned to die will be executed (all fifty-five cases in California have been overturned), it will cost four point five million dollars to execute one felon in California, and seven point three million dollars in New York.

"Nor can these costs be significantly lowered. Since each trial is unique, and most of the costs are incurred in the trial phase — not on appeal — there really is no economy of scale. The four point five million figures do not include appeals that average only a hundred thousand. When a defendant faces a possible death sentence, more time is spent investigating the facts of the case, more pretrial motions are filed, the trial tends to last much longer, more expert witnesses are called to testify, and there are, of course, many legal objections and appeals. Most of all, there is no cost-saving plea bargaining when the prosecution seeks the death penalty.

"Because of the Supreme Court's rulings, there is no way to streamline this elaborate process. Any attempt to do so would deny a defendant the protections guaranteed under the Constitution and increase the possibility of sending innocent people to their death. And the recent decision in the case of Alvin Ford — that a condemned man is entitled to a court hearing on the question of his mental competence before he can be executed — can only further the delays and increase the costs. Like it or not, the Supreme Court has made it abundantly clear that shortcuts to justice are legally unacceptable.

"Nationally, the average offender who is sentenced to death is about thirty years old. Let's say he lives to seventy — forty more years. At twenty thousand dollars a year to keep him in prison that adds up to eighty thousand. Indeed, if all people charged with capital offenses were actually sentenced to death, then the death penalty would be slightly cheaper in some states. But, in California, for example, only one out of ten is sentenced to death — so ninety percent of the cases bear the costs of both a capital trial and life imprisonment.

"It isn't necessary to be an accountant to realize that if you substitute life imprisonment for the death penalty, you will save almost five hundred thousand dollars per trial for the first degree murder in California, and one point eight million in New York. And since there are about two hundred fifty such trials in California, the abolition of the death penalty would save the taxpayers about one hundred twenty-five million dollars a year. In New York it has been estimated to be seventy-five million. Put another way, the death penalty consumes a disproportionate share of our criminal justice dollars.

"Not even the most avid supporters of the death penalty wants to execute people capriciously. But the costs incurred in easing our doubts and assuring fairness in capital cases have now reached the point at which they constitute eloquent testimony in their own right. Until scholarly research can prove the death penalty is more cost effective in deterring murder than life imprisonment, we think that our elected officials might do well to choose the cheaper option.

"For almost a year I had been studying the history of capital punishment with emphasis on the various methods of execution. I concluded that we had taken most of the gore and horror out of the ultimate penalty. We no longer execute in public, nor do we still regard the infliction of pain and degradation as a necessary part of capital punishment. Lethal injection seemed to be a major advance. It virtually eliminated the gore, but, as I soon found out, none of the horror.

"I had led myself to believe that death by lethal injection was a nonevent. The condemned man would drift off to sleep like a hospital patient who had received general anesthesia. Lethal injection was supposed to mitigate the horror of execution. Andy Barefoot, a 39-year-old former oil field roughneck who was convicted in nineteen seventy-eight for the murder of a Texas policeman, was supposed to die a painless and humane death, if not with dignity at least without shame or horror.

"When I entered the death chamber at midnight Barefoot was already strapped to a hospital gurney. Tubes were stuck in both his arms. Saline solution flowed through his veins. He looked up and managed a smile. I had expected that he would be asleep or heavily sedated. He was alert and wide awake. I was scared.

"Barefoot did not look like his picture. He was smaller. I had expected a powerful man. The psychiatrist had labelled him a dangerous felon, a prerequisite for execution in Texas, one who was likely to kill again. He looked like a petty criminal.

"I was ashamed, ashamed for being there and afraid that he would ask something of me. I was an intruder, the only member of the public who had trespassed on his private moment of anguish. In my face he could see the horror of his death.

"The death chamber was brightly lit like a hospital operating room or a television studio. The brick walls were freshly painted a powder blue. It was air-conditioned cold. The tubes came out of a square hole in the wall. The executioner hid behind a one-way mirror.

"Warden Jack Pursley began by asking the condemned if he had any last words. Barefoot strained to hold his head up. Turning toward us, he said: 'I hope that one day we can look back on the evil that we are doing right now like we do the witches when they were burned at the stake.' After saying that he had prayed all day for the widow of the policeman he had been convicted of killing, Barefoot added: 'I want everybody to know I hold nothing against them for anything that they're doing to me. I forgive them all. I'm sorry for anything I've ever done to anybody.'

"When Barefoot finished, Pursley gave the signal: 'We are ready.' In the adjacent room an unidentified executioner squeezed a syringe containing the lethal drugs, but nothing happened. The intravenous tubes were ten feet long.

"Barefoot began to talk, asking that we say goodbye to his friends for him. As he began listing the names of several death row inmates, Barefoot let out a terrible gasp. His neck straightened. His eyes bulged and his back arched. He lay stiff on the gurney, glazed eyes fixed on the ceiling, like a soldier standing at attention.

"Four minutes passed before the medical examiner pronounced Thomas Andy Barefoot dead. He tried to close Barefoot's eyes, but the lids would not budge. He tried a second time. Still they would not move. Finally the doctor said: 'Eyes dilated, respiration stopped, heartbeat slowed. Barefoot is dead.' I thought to myself, no he isn't. His heart is still beating.

"We were marched out of the death chamber and down the long corridor of the visiting room. When we reached the outside of the prison the flood lights came on. There were television cameras and microphones. The crowd, mostly students from a nearby university, started cheering. I was not prepared for the celebration. Some people had on Halloween costumes. One was dressed as an executioner, with a black silk hood pulled over his head. He was holding a cardboard axe.

"There are many Barefoots on death row nationwide. What method will be used to execute them? The superiority of lethal injection lies in its cleanliness and lack of dramatic appeal. It is the only method that allows us to envision the dead man as having entered an eternal, peaceful sleep. Indeed, the sleep metaphor, most often expressed in the phrase, 'putting him to sleep' implies that the execution is for the condemned's own good as well as a benefit to society. It is the way we explain the loss of a pet to children.

"If we are serious about using the death penalty as a deterrent or even to seek retribution, then we ought to make executions public once again. Those who believe in the deterrent or retributive value of the death penalty should be pleased to recapture the object lessons of the nineteenth century. Those who oppose capital punishment should welcome the opportunity to expose the execution ceremony for the inhumane and anachronistic ritual that it has become. At the very least, public executions would force us to face directly the consequences of our decision to kill those who have killed. Over seventy percent of Americans now say that they favor capital punishment, but how many of them are prepared for one hundred fifty executions a month? Not many we suppose."

Eight

The Execution of Juvenile Offenders

James Terry Roach was convicted and sentenced to death for the deaths of 16-year-old Tommy Taylor and his 14-year-old girlfriend, Carlotta Hartness, in Columbia, South Carolina.

Roach was 17 at the time of the crime, and had an I.Q. measured at 64. On the advice of his court-appointed attorney, Roach pled guilty to the crime and was sentenced to death by a Circuit Court judge. No evidence of his age or mental capacity was presented. There were two co-defendants: Ronnie Mahaffey, a 16-year-old who was sentenced to life in prison after agreeing to testify against the others, and Joseph Carl Shaw, 22, the ringleader of the group. Shaw was also sentenced to death.

Roach's execution drew international attention as the first non-consensual execution of a juvenile offender since the death penalty was reinstated in 1976. South Carolina Governor Richard Riley received pleas for clemency from former President Jimmy Carter, Mother Theresa, the secretary general of the United Nations, and others.

In December of 1985 a complaint on Roach's behalf was filed with the Inter-American Commission on Human Rights on the grounds that his execution would violate United States obligations under international customary law and the human rights charter of the Organization of American States. The Commission urged Governor Riley to postpone the execution until the complaint could be reviewed. Riley refused. Several months after the execution, the OAS issued a decision declaring the execution of juveniles to be a violation of international law.

There are currently 32 juveniles on U.S. death rows. Some were as young as 15 at the time of their crimes. The Supreme Court is considering whether the execution of juveniles violates the Eighth Amendment.

Nine

The Execution of
Vietnam Veterans

Wayne Felde was convicted and sentenced to death for the 1978 killing of a Shreveport, Louisiana, police officer. While there was no question of Felde's guilt in the case, significant debate about his culpability has been raised.

Felde voluntarily joined the army and was sent to Vietnam in 1969. When he returned to the States he was suffering from nightmares, flashbacks and other symptoms of a disease now recognized by the American Medical Association as Post-Traumatic Stress Disorder (PTSD). The disorder is blamed in similar symptoms in over half a million Vietnam veterans, and is treatable. But when Felde returned, the disease had not yet been recognized, and Felde received no treatment.

Testimony at Felde's trial strongly suggested that Felde was attempting to commit suicide when the victim tried to wrestle the gun away. In the struggle, the gun went off, fatally injuring the officer.

Felde's trial attorney based his defense of Felde on his symptoms of PTSD. But the defense, the first of its kind in the United States, failed. After his conviction, both Felde and his attorney asked the jury for a death sentence. The jury tearfully obliged, returning a death sentence with the following statement: "We feel the trial of Wayne Felde has brought to the forefront those extreme stress disorders prevalent among thousands of our veterans."

PTSD is now a recognized and treatable illness. Just two weeks after Felde's execution, the California Supreme Court unanimously overturned the death sentence of a death row prisoner in that state, citing the presence of PTSD.

Ten

Marie Deans

"I am the death penalty legal defense coordinator in Virginia. Under grants from law schools and the Virginia Law Foundation, I track all death cases, assist and provide resources to appointed attorneys, whether private or public defenders. I recruit volunteer attorneys to represent those under the sentence of death and serve as coordinator of these cases.

"In the last five executions in Virginia, I have been in the death house with the men until a few minutes before they were killed. I am also a member of a murder victim's family, and I am the founder of a national organization, most of whom do work similar to mine or work in states with no death penalty to be sure those states remain abolitionist. We do this work because we have been there. We know what murder leaves behind, and we deeply resent cheap, emotional, unknowing support of a penalty which likely creates additional families like ours and blocks efforts to find effective solutions. We resent our pain being exploited to support this red herring.

"One evening in the middle of last March, my husband and I watched a young man standing outside an Illinois courtroom lean toward a phalanx of microphones and speak openly of revenge. Inside the courtroom John Wayne Gacy had just been sentenced to death for killing, among others, this man's young brother. He was an honest young man, speaking honest emotions about a monster who had tortured and murdered thirty-three young boys. One of the saddest factors in murder is how quickly the victim is forgotten. After the first few days, the attention of the media shifts from the murdered to the murderer. The murdered becomes a statistic, while the murderer becomes an individual who will be remembered. We remember Gary Gilmore, John Spenkelink and Jesse Bishop. Do we remember the names of those they killed?

38

"My husband and I understood so well what the young man on TV was feeling and we felt an intense sympathy for him. Eight and a half years ago, my husband's mother was shot to death by an escaped convict.

"Murder is not like any other death. A little over a year before my husband's mother was killed, his father had died from cancer. At fifty-four, he had been a relatively young man, and his death, after two years of illness, had come hard to all of us. But we knew how to react. We knew how to grieve, how to handle our emotions. Friends and neighbors knew how to help us. Our culture has given us a ritual of mourning and remembrance and taught us how to accept death in every way it comes to us — except murder.

"How do you react to death by murder? How do you separate the death itself from the violence of the murder? While murder has always been a part of society, it is taboo, and taboo implies complicity. The victim's family has been drawn into an act that has brought consciousness to the subliminal terror of society out of control. Society's determination to push back the terror and enforce order takes precedence over the death. The ritual of revenge takes precedence over the ritual of mourning and remembrance.

"Would it not be better if we spent more time and energy mourning the death and remembering the life? When we concentrate on the killer to the exclusion of his victims, do we not wound our own sense of humanity? When we make the killer a celebrity, do we not encourage the deranged to seek out innocent victims in order to obtain immortality? And most importantly, what are we teaching our children about the value we place on human life?

"Long before his mother was killed, my husband and I had asked ourselves these questions, and slowly we found ourselves in opposition to the death penalty. My mother-in-law's violent death and the months that followed strengthened that opposition.

"The violence of my mother-in-law's murder was taking over our lives. I was five months pregnant and began hemorrhaging. For my husband, that marked the end of our complicity. Not only was his mother a victim, now he was seeing his entire family turned into victims. He went to the prosecutor's office and told him what was happening to our family. He said he would fight any attempt to bring the man back to this state to be tried for murder with a possible penalty of death. The prosecutor in New England was seeking a sentence of life in prison and the prosecutor here agreed that, if that was the sentence, our primary concern, that no one else become a victim, would be answered, and there would be no need for extradition.

"It has been difficult for many people to understand my husband's decision. We both felt that the man had to be captured before he hurt or killed anyone else and we were grateful to those who had worked long, hard hours on the investigation. We were fully aware of the man's past record and our family spent cooperating with the police and prosecutors in our home state and New England. We had carried out our responsibilities to our family and ourselves.

"For four months we went through the complicated procedures of saving an endangered pregnancy. All our energies and thoughts were concentrated on the baby. When our son was born, the family rejoiced. He was well and whole and wonderful.

"Babies bring the future with them. They also bring the past, and the joy he brought was tingled with sadness. He constantly brought back memories of his grandparents to us.

"We will always remember the night she was murdered and the months that followed, but we have been able to separate them from her death and, therefore, from her life. We believe that separation was possible because we did not become involved in the course of the death penalty.

"The violence of murder is abhorrent; but the long sequence of trials and appeals that ultimately leads to another killing is not a solution but a process of carrying on that violence and while it goes on the family lives a day-to-day existence focused on the death of their loved one. It is as if the body were being kept in the front parlor, preserved and waiting to be buried. The catharsis of mourning is delayed while the tension and pain continue to build. It is no wonder that some families of victims begin to cry out for revenge, no wonder that they believe only the death of the murderer will release them from their living nightmare. Through no fault of his own, the young man on TV had been caught up in that process. Will he ever be able to separate his own life from the violence begun by John Wayne Gacy and carried on by society?

"It is not easy to tell a story like ours, but I believe it is easier for us than it will ever be for this young man. In response to the pain of his brother's death, society was prepared to offer him nothing but revenge. Somehow we must find a better, more humane way to deal with murder, a way that does not twist sorrow into vengeance and memory into nightmares.

"While you may rationalize a difference between state killing and individual killing, calling one murder and one execution, we know that the impact on both families is the same. If there is a difference it is that for the families of those who are killed by the state, it is worse, for they have to watch and wait helplessly as their loved one faces a predetermined death date. They live for years anticipating a killing and then living through it and then they live with the aftermath. God knows what all that aftermath will entail.

"Punishment only for the sake of punishment, whether it is strip searching a man's mother for a non-contact visit or killing a select group of prisoners, dehumanizes the punisher as well as the punished. In the case of the death penalty, we are all the punisher."

Eleven

Racism and the Death Penalty

Willie Darden was sentenced to death for the murder of furniture store owner Carl Turman during a robbery at the store in Lakeland, Florida.

Darden proclaimed his innocence from the moment of his arrest until the moment of his execution over 14 years later. There remains significant doubt of Darden's guilt.

Darden was tried by an all-white jury in Inverness, Florida, a county with a history of racial segregation and oppression. The prosecutor's opening remarks to prospective jurors in the trial demonstrated the racial climate of the era:

"The testimony is going to show I think very shortly when the trial starts that the victims in this case were white, and of course Mr. Darden, the defendant, is black. Can each of you tell me you can try Mr. Darden as if he was white?"

Throughout the trial, the prosecutor characterized Darden as subhuman, saying such things as, "Willie Darden is an animal who should be placed on a leash." The United States Supreme Court sharply criticized this misconduct, but refused to find that it unfairly influenced the trial.

In the face of evidence that those who kill whites in Florida are nearly five times more likely to be sentenced to death than those who kill blacks, the prosecution of Willie Darden becomes the story of a man who may well have been innocent, but whose protestations were overshadowed by the skin color of his victim and himself.

Twelve

Ineffective
Trial Representation

John Young was executed for the murder of three elderly people during the commission of a robbery. Young had beaten six people, three of whom died of their injuries.

Young's childhood history goes a long way to explaining his violent behavior as an adult. When John was four or five years old, his mother was murdered as she lay in bed with John and his brother beside her. The mother was shot twice with a double-barreled shotgun. After his mother's death, John was taken to live with his grandmother. She and his uncles were alcoholics and bootleggers. They quickly decided that they didn't want responsibility for Young and his brothers and sisters, and the children were shuffled from relative to relative over the next ten years.

Young was appointed an attorney for his capital trial. The attorney, Charles Marchman, had his own problems. According to an affidavit signed by Marchman shortly before Young's execution, he was heavily involved with drugs and undergoing severe family problems during the time he was representing Young.

Marchman separated from his wife in March of 1975, in part because he was having a homosexual relationship with a man in Macon, Georgia. In late 1975 Marchman took responsibility for caring for his elderly father, who lived in Tennessee. He traveled there frequently, and became increasingly less involved with his legal work. He admitted to spending little time on Young's defense.

Marchman admits that he never obtained any social history from Young or his relatives. He limited his trial preparations to the guilt-phase, and to finding a single psychologist to testify during the sentencing phase. Young's jury never heard any testimony about his childhood.

43

Three weeks after the Young trial, Marchman was arrested for possession of marijuana and intent to distribute other drugs. He was sentenced to jail and was later disbarred. When he was released from jail, Marchman went virtually underground. Appellate attorneys for Young were unable to find him to discuss the case. Marchman did not come forward about the Young case until 1985, ten years after the trial. Only then did he admit to having represented Young at trial with almost no preparation. Marchman pleaded with an appellate judge to grant Young's request for a hearing on trial incompetence. The plea was refused. John Young died.

Thirteen

Execution by Default

Robert Streetman was convicted and sentenced to death for the 1982 murder of Christine Baker of Kountze, Texas, who was shot in the head while she sat in her home.

Streetman's death sentence was imposed under a part of the Texas death penalty statute that is currently under challenge at the United States Supreme Court. That challenge (*Franklin v. Lynaugh*) may require new sentencing hearings for a majority of those on Texas' death row. With the exception of Streetman's, all executions in Texas have been halted pending the Court's decision in *Franklin*.

Under Supreme Court rules, four votes are needed to win full review of a petitioner's case, or to hold a petition while the Court decides a similar issue. Five votes are needed to grant a stay of execution. When Streetman's execution date was set, the Court had agreed to hear *Franklin,* under which Streetman appealed to the Court. That is, four members of the Court had agreed to hear the *Franklin* case. On the night of the execution, the Court voted 4–4, agreeing to hold Streetman's case until *Franklin* was decided. But when presented with the petition for a stay, the Court was also split 4–4, and the stay was therefore denied. After Streetman's death, the Court rescinded their decision to hear the case, declaring the issue moot because of the petitioner's death.

Fourteen

Executions Despite the Wishes of Prosecutors and Victims' Families

Kenneth Brock was executed in Texas for the murder of a 7-11 manager during the course of a robbery.

Both the prosecutor who convicted Brock, and the family of Michael Sedita, the murder victim, asked for clemency for Brock. The prosecutor testified that Brock had been a good prisoner while on death row, and that he no longer considered the death penalty appropriate for Brock's crime.

J.M. Sedita, the father of the victim, in testimony before the Pardons and Parole Board, said, in part: "Killing Kenneth Brock is wrong. It will not change what has happened to my son. It will not ease my suffering or the suffering of my wife. Two wrongs do not make a right. I could not be at peace if Kenneth Brock dies."

Despite these pleas, the Pardons and Parole Board and the governor's office refused to grant clemency to Brock.

Fifteen

Botched Executions

John Louis Evans was sentenced to death for the robbery of a pawn shop in 1977 during which the shop owner was shot and killed. He was the first person to be electrocuted in Alabama in 18 years.

On April 22, 1983, with over 30 witnesses, Evans, head shaven and smeared with conducting gel, was strapped into the Alabama electric chair. He was given a 30-second surge of 1,900 volts of electricity.

According to witnesses: "A fiery arc shot from beneath the mask that covered his face. Smoke poured from the electrode on his left leg," (*Times* magazine April 2, 1983). The strap on Evans' leg burned loose. After the initial surge, physicians examined Evans and found that his heart continued to beat. One witness reported seeing Evans struggle to take a breath. The warden gave the signal that a second surge of electricity be given to Evans, but dropped a curtain in front of the witness booth, shutting out view of the continuing execution. Officials replaced the strap on Evans' leg, tightened each of the straps, and a second surge of electricity was administered a full four and a half minutes after the first. Evans was still alive. His attorneys made a final appeal for the execution to be halted. A phone call was made to then–Governor George Wallace, pleading that the execution had become intolerably cruel and unusual and asking for intervention. The Governor refused, and a third, and this time fatal, surge of electricity was given to Evans. The time between the first surge of electricity and pronouncement of Evans' death was 14 minutes.

The botched execution caused an outcry across the state and nation. The forensic lab which conducted an autopsy on Evans showed that his body had two fourth degree burns on the temple and a second degree burn on the leg. The Prison Commissioner denied that the execution had gone awry.

The gas chamber at San Quentin prison was the scene of particularly horrifying executions in the past. Witnesses reported seeing condemned prisoners being dragged or carried screaming into the death chamber. One prisoner cut his throat with a piece of glass and was taken into the chamber bleeding profusely. He managed to free his arm, which was slippery with blood, from one of the restraining straps and died shouting and struggling to free the other arm. This was a double execution and the other prisoner sat strapped to the chair beside him.

Sixteen

Hugo Bedau

Hugo Bedau is considered by many to be America's most knowledgeable expert on capital punishment. A Harvard Ph.D., he is a member of the Philosophy Department at Tufts University in Medford, Massachusetts. He was born in Portland, Oregon, in 1926 and during the second World War served in the United States Naval Reserve.

Bedau is the author or editor of four books on the death penalty: *The Death Penalty in America; Capital Punishment in the United States; The Courts, the Constitution and Capital Punishment;* and *Death Is Different.* With Michael Radelet he coauthored a book-length law review essay, "Miscarriages of Justice in Potentially Capital Cases."

He presented oral arguments before the United States Supreme Court on death penalty cases in 1972, 1975 and 1976.

He has done research projects on capital punishment funded by four different private and government foundations and has spoken before various professional and scientific groups in regard to the death penalty.

"I oppose the death sentence for several reasons. I think that one of the most significant things I have learned from the study of capital punishment is the way in which the criminal law visits harsh penalties, the harshest of all, death, in an unfair way. History has shown that capital punishment has never been applied fairly.

"It is extremely hard to draw up reasons why it is fair to kill the murderer who kills seven people, and not the person who kills just one person. You make one exception and you end up widening it. Exceptions, the more one thinks about them, begin to be arbitrary.

"Some states have the death penalty for cop killers. I don't feel we should make exceptions in favor of the police. If the police get special treatment, why not firemen? Everyone's life is equally important. Why should the police get this kind of special vindication or revenge if they are killed on the job?

"I see little proof that capital punishment is a successful deterrent, because it has been around throughout recorded history in one way or another yet murders and other crimes continue to occur. It's true we don't know how many people have not been deterred. We don't really have a perfect account of all the murders that have taken place.

"But it's also true that we don't know how many innocent people have been sentenced to death and executed.

"Capital punishment is simply judicial murder. It is the dignified exercise of the state power to extinguish the life of one of its members. When that's done by private individuals, that's murder, and it's a crime.

"In the past sixty years in this country about half a million criminal homicides have been committed, but only about four thousand executions, all but fifty of which were men. If we could be assured that the four thousand persons executed were the worst of the worst, repeat offenders without exception, the most dangerous murderers in captivity — the ones who had killed more than once and were likely to kill again, and the least likely to be confined in prison without imminent danger to other inmates and the staff — then one might accept half a million murders and a few thousand executions with a sense that rough justice had been done.

"But the truth is otherwise. Persons are sentenced to death and executed not because they have been found to be uncontrollably violent, hopelessly poor parole and release risks, or for other reasons. Instead, they are executed for entirely different reasons. They have a poor defense at trial; they have no funds to bring sympathetic witnesses to court; they are immigrants or strangers in the community where they were tried; the prosecuting attorney wants the publicity that goes with sending a killer to the chair; they have inexperienced or overworked counsel at trial; there are no funds for an appeal or for a transcript of the trial record; they are members of a despised racial minority. In short, the actual study of why particular persons have been sentenced to death and executed does not show any careful winnowing of the worst from the bad.

"It shows instead that the executed were usually the unlucky victims of prejudice and discrimination, the losers in an arbitrary lottery that could just as well have spared them as killed them, the victims of the disadvantages that almost always go with poverty. A system like this does not enhance respect for human life; it cheapens and degrades it. However heinous murder and other crimes are, the system of capital punishment does not compensate for or erase those crimes. It only tends to add new injuries of its own to the catalogue of our inhumanity to each other.

"Michael Radelet and I found three hundred fifty cases in which defendants convicted of capital or potentially capital crimes in this century, and in many cases sentenced to death, have later been found to be innocent. Out of those three hundred fifty cases, twenty-three of them were executed. Our total of twenty-three wrongful executions is not an estimate, and it cannot serve as a basis for a reasonable estimate of the total number of wrongful executions in the United States during this century. Estimating the extent of the problem of convicting the innocent in potentially capital cases by extrapolation from our data is not possible. The cases in our catalogue are only a nonrandom subset of an indeterminate number of the relevant cases. The full story of *all* cases disposed of by an execution must be examined before such an estimate would be possible. Of the seven thousand executions in this country since 1900, we examined only a hundred or so. Our findings prompt us to echo the words of an earlier investigator who noted that the catalogue of erroneous convictions 'could be extended, but if what has already been presented fails to convince the reader of the fallibility of human judgment then nothing will.'

"In virtually every year in this century, in some jurisdiction or other, at least one person has been under death sentence who was later proved to be innocent. Based on this evidence, it is virtually certain that at least some of the nearly two thousand men and women currently under sentence of death in this country are innocent.

"It is useful in the broad context to recognize that many such cases of incipient error do occur. No doubt the risk of executing the innocent grows as the risks of arresting, indicting, and trying the innocent also grows. The risk that really matters is the risk of erroneous conviction. It is also true that the risk of convicting the innocent is increased so long as due process errors are committed and uncorrected. But involuntary confessions, perjured testimony, planted circumstantial evidence, and other errors and mistakes are irrelevant for the purposes of our study except when they play a role in securing the conviction of an innocent defendant.

"Miscarriages of justice are caused by a wide variety of factors. Some involve the decision by the police and prosecution to seek a conviction of the defendant despite lack of firm belief that he is guilty. Some are the result of negligence on the part of the authorities. Others are the product of well-intentioned error that anyone might make.

"In a few instances, a convincing record indicates that the defendants were victims of what can only be described as a 'frame-up.' Some of the most notorious—such as the nineteen fifteen case of Joe Hill, and the nineteen sixteen Mooney-Billings case—were part of the pitched battles fought by employers earlier this century against union organizers. Mooney and Billings were eventually cleared and released, but Hill was executed. In two other famous cases—the Sacco-Vanzetti case, and the Hauptmann case—the convictions, death sentences, and executions were achieved by a large cast of characters, probably never systematically orchestrated into a frame-up in quite the manner that was done in the Hill and Mooney-Billings cases. In other lesser known cases where error was knowingly perpetrated by the police or the prosecutors, or both working together, the magnitude of the corruption of justice may have been as great as in the Hill and Mooney-Billings cases.

"Clear injustices perpetrated by the police compose nearly a quarter of the errors we have identified, and perhaps not surprisingly they were usually coerced confessions. In forty-nine percent of the cases, the confession was later shown to have been coerced.

"In nineteen twenty-four, Hardy was convicted in Michigan largely on the basis of testimony against him that was later proved to have been provided by a witness who had tried to testify in his favor, only to be discouraged from doing so by police threats.

"In nineteen sixty-one, also in Michigan, Clark, Hall, and Kuykendall were convicted of murder and sentenced to life imprisonment. A year later, the chief witness against them admitted she had lied at the trial because the police had promised her lenient treatment for another crime if she would implicate these three defendants. In twenty-two of our cases, this type of improper conduct by the police helped to bring about a wrongful conviction.

"Overzealous prosecutorial tactics are not limited to suppression of exculpatory evidence. Sometimes the prosecutor will stoop to the introduction of fraudulent incriminating evidence, as in the nineteen thirty-three Fisher case in New York. William was convicted and sentenced to prison largely on the basis of a gun offered in evidence—a gun the prosecutor knew had not been fired by the defendant. Other times the police and prosecutor may manage to discredit unfairly a witness who might otherwise have come to the aid of the defense.

"There is no common or typical route by which an innocent defendant can be vindicated, and vindication, if it ever comes, will not necessarily come in time to benefit the defendant. The criminal justice system is not designed to scrutinize its own decisions for a wide range of factual errors once a conviction has been obtained. Our data show that it is rare for anyone within the system to play the decisive role in correcting error. Even when actors in the system do get involved, they often do so on their own time and without official support or encouragement. Far more commonly, the efforts of persons on the fringe of the system, or even wholly outside it, make the difference. The coincidences involved in exposing so many of the errors and the luck that is so often required suggest that only a fraction of the wrongly convicted are eventually able to clear their names.

"Many innocent defendants have used the system, notably the appellate courts, to win their freedom. But in the bulk of the cases, the defendant has been vindicated not because of the system, but in spite of it. Most victims of miscarriage, like other felony defendants found guilty, have expended all their financial resources trying to avoid conviction. Once convicted and imprisoned, few have attorneys who are willing or able to continue to fight for them. In short, the lesson taught by our data is how lucky these erroneously convicted defendants were to have been eventually cleared.

"To think that these cases show that the system works is to ignore the fact that, once a defendant is convicted, there is no system to which he can turn and on which he can rely to verify and rectify substantive error. The convicted defendant can initiate an appeal based on procedural error in his trial, or on newly discovered evidence, but not on his factual guilt or innocence. This leaves most erroneously convicted defendants with no place to turn for vindication.

"Next to establishing that no crime occurred, perhaps the most convincing disclosure of error occurs in cases where the actual perpetrator intervenes. This happened in forty-seven of our cases. The true offender confessed on his or her deathbed. In a few cases, the true offender was the innocent man's codefendant, and exoneration came when the codefendant confessed. In a few others, a person already in prison for another crime, confessed his guilt to a previous crime for which the wrong man had been convicted, and this conviction was verified.

"I must repeat that Radelet and I have not, nor has anyone else, examined all of the more than seven thousand executions during this century in light of all the available evidence. Until this is done, proposing trends in the execution of the innocent is idle speculation.

"In Florida charges against Joseph Green Brown were dropped and he was released after spending nearly 13 years on death row, and once coming to within fifteen hours of being executed. The state had made a secret deal with its chief witness to testify at Brown's nineteen seventy-four trial. Eight months after the trial this witness admitted that he lied, but it was not until nineteen eighty-six that the Eleventh Circuit Court of Appeals voided the conviction, ruling that the prosecutor had knowingly allowed the witness to lie and mislead the jurors in his closing argument.

"Earl Johnson was executed in Mississippi on May twentieth, nineteen eighty-seven. Johnson was convicted of killing a police officer, who was in the process of investigating an assault. The victim of the assault initially said that Johnson was not the man who assaulted her, but Johnson confessed to the murder. He immediately claimed that the confession had been given only after the police had threatened him and his grandparents with physical violence. The assault victim then changed her story and implicated Johnson.

"In Pennsylvania in nineteen forty-seven, David Almeida and his codefendant were engaged in the armed robbery of a supermarket. A police officer was killed while attempting to apprehend them. Later evidence proved that the fatal bullet was not fired by Almeida, or even by one of his cofelons, but by another police officer. Nevertheless, Almeida was convicted of murder and sentenced to death. On appeal his conviction was overturned.

"In nineteen seventy-five, Jerry Banks of Georgia was convicted on two counts of murder and sentenced to death. The conviction was reversed on appeal on the ground that the prosecution knowingly withheld evidence. In nineteen seventy-six, Banks was retried, reconvicted, and resentenced to death. Appellate courts refused to vacate this conviction. His attorney was later disbarred. In nineteen eighty, a third trial was ordered because of newly discovered evidence. Part of this evidence came from a previously silent witness, whose testimony revealed that the fatal shots could not have come from Banks' weapon. Banks was released later that year when all charges against him were dismissed by a circuit court judge. Three months later, after he learned his wife wanted a divorce, Banks killed her and himself. In nineteen eighty-three, a suit against the county for mishandling the case was filed by Banks' three children, and the county agreed to pay them one hundred fifty thousand dollars.

"In nineteen eighty-three, Anthony Brown from Florida was convicted of first degree murder and sentenced to death, despite a jury recommendation of life imprisonment. The only evidence against Brown was from the testimony of a codefendant, who was sentenced to life for his role in the crime. On appeal, the conviction was reversed and a new trial was ordered because Brown had not been notified before the state took a crucial deposition in the case and had thereby been deprived of his right to confront and cross-examine an adverse witness. At retrial in nineteen eighty-six, the codefendant admitted that his incrimination of Brown at the first trial had been perjured, and Brown was acquitted.

"In nineteen eighty-two Neil Ferber from Pennsylvania was convicted of first degree murder and sentenced to death. In nineteen eighty-six, at the urging of the district attorney, the trial judge ordered a new trial. A polygraph test indicated that state's star witness against Ferber, a former cellmate, had perjured himself at the trial, falsely claiming that Ferber had confessed to the crimes. An earlier polygraph test, administered before trial and with the same results, had not been revealed to the defense. A homicide detective and several other prosecutors were also convinced of Ferber's innocence, and an eyewitness to the crime was positive that Ferber was not the man she saw. Two months after the new trial was ordered, charges against Ferber were formally dropped.

"In Idaho, nineteen sixty-two, Gerald Anderson confessed to the murders of two neighbors. Anderson was in jail for ten months, although his confession was the only evidence against him. It later became evident that the confession had been obtained by coercion. Meanwhile, another man confessed and was tried and convicted of the crimes.

"In North Carolina in nineteen forty-two William Wellman, a black man convicted of raping a white woman, was sentenced to death. He was spared when the governor became convinced that Wellman's alibi claim was really true. After Wellman's conviction, evidence was obtained that proved he was hundreds of miles from the scene of the crime and that the conviction was based on mistaken identity.

"Paul Dwyer, whose home was in Maine, was arrested in New Jersey in nineteen thirty-seven, after a routine search of his car revealed the bodies of two murder victims. He was held incommunicado, pleaded guilty, and was convicted. In prison Dwyer protested his innocence, claiming that a deputy sheriff in Maine had threatened to murder his mother unless he secretly disposed of the two bodies. A year later, after investigation of Dwyer's charges, the sheriff was indicted, convicted, and sentenced to prison. Dwyer, although cleared, was not released from prison until nineteen fifty-nine.

"Two recent decisions by the Supreme Court indicate that it does not judge the risk of wrongful conviction to be so great as to warrant certain minor modifications in the imposition of the death penalty. Requiring a unanimous jury vote to impose a death sentence is one procedure that would reduce the probability of wrongful executions but in nineteen eighty-four, the Court, in upholding the constitutionality of Florida's jury-override provision, rejected an effort to require a simple majority vote, and thus is likely to demand a unanimous jury verdict to impose a death sentence. Also, several studies have found that the exclusion from capital juries of citizens who stand opposed to the death penalty makes such juries more conviction prone and sympathetic to the prosecution. Nevertheless, in nineteen eighty-six the Court refused to prohibit the exclusion of such jurors.

"Evaluating the argument against the death penalty based on the fact that innocent defendants have been and will be executed requires some care. As it is certain that there are and will be such cases, death penalty proponents cannot evade the problem. Ernest van den Haag, one of this country's most vocal death penalty proponents, agrees, but then argues that the benefits of capital punishment outweigh this liability.

"Van den Haag's defense of the death penalty, despite his concession that some innocent defendants will be executed, can be criticized on grounds other than the impossibility of performing the calculations his argument requires. One could accept his cost-benefit logic for the sake of the argument, and still point to at least three objections. First, there is little or no empirical evidence on behalf of any of the alleged benefits of the death penalty that make it superior to long term imprisonment.

"Second, van den Haag's comparison of the death penalty with other activities that cause the death of the innocent (building houses, driving a car, playing golf or football) is misleading for two reasons. Those who participate in the latter voluntarily consent to their exposure to risk, whereas there is no reason to believe that the innocent defendant has consented to the risk of being executed. Furthermore, the intention of capital punishment is to kill the convicted, whereas this is not the intention of the practices to which van den Haag draws a parallel.

"Third, and most importantly, we need to consider basic issues of individual rights in a democratic society. We suspect that those who reason as van den Haag does might see the issue differently were they the innocent defendants facing the executioner.

"Capital punishment is cruel and unusual. It is a relic of the earliest days of penology, when slavery, branding, and other corporal punishments were commonplace. Like those other barbaric practices, it has no place in a civilized society.

"There is an alternative to capital punishment: long-term imprisonment. Such a punishment is retributive and can be made appropriately severe to reflect the gravity of the crime for which it is the punishment. It gives adequate (though hardly perfect) protection to the public. It is free of the worst defect to which the death penalty is liable: execution of the innocent. It tacitly acknowledges that there is no way for a criminal, alive or dead, to make amends for murder or other grave crimes against the person. Finally, it has symbolic significance. The death penalty, more than any other kind of killing, is done in the name of society and on its behalf. Each of us has a hand in such a killing. Thus, abolishing the death penalty represents extending the hand of life even to those who by their crimes have "forfeited" any right to live. It is a tacit admission that we must abandon the folly and pretense of attempting to secure perfect justice in an imperfect world.

"Searching for an epigram suitable for our times in which governments have launched vast campaigns of war and suppression of internal dissent with methods that can only be described as savage and criminal, Albert Camus was prompted to admonish: 'Let us be neither victims nor executioners.' Perhaps better than any other, this exhortation points the way between forbidden extremes."

Seventeen

Victor Streib

Victor Streib is a professor at Cleveland-Marshall College of Law at Cleveland State University who does research on violent crime by juveniles, and violent crimes by women.

"I started working on the juvenile question in the mid-seventies. Most of my present research is on the women on death row. I'm working on a book on that now and my past work was on the juveniles. I wrote a book called *Death Penalty for Juveniles* [Indiana University Press, 1987] a while back and I try to keep the research up to date on that.

"The number of persons currently under juvenile death sentences has dropped to the lowest point since nineteen eighty-three when I first began recording the data. As of February, nineteen eighty-nine, twenty-seven persons are on death row for crimes committed while under the age of eighteen, the most typical age cutoff for juvenile court. These twenty-seven condemned juveniles constitute only one-point-two percent of the total number of persons on death row.

"I'm also an attorney and represent kids and women on death row. I represent Paula Cooper in Indiana right now. She's a woman and also a juvenile on death row. I think of myself mostly as a researcher even though I do represent those on death row.

Most of these kids have had a difficult background. Dorothy Lewis's research found that most all those on death row came from very abusive homes. There are some who did not come from such a background and in fact came from a good home. I think it's not always the single family, the poverty, but that they've seen violence in their families that contributes to their being on death row. They get the message very clearly that violence is the way to solve their problems. Then when they want to solve their problems, they use violence.

"Almost all of the juveniles on death row have had court-appointed attorneys. They had public defenders at trial and if they are on death row, they have to get an attorney to handle the appeals. In most of the states the public defender cannot take the case beyond the trial level. Then they have to get a new public defender for the state appeal and after the state appeal is through, and they're getting ready to go on into Federal courts, then the state public defender can't work for them any longer. So they are left without any lawyer at all. At that point, in order to go with their appeals, it's very hard to find lawyers for them.

"The state paid public defenders are not allowed to represent anyone in anything other than a state action. Trying to find lawyers to represent them in Federal action is very hard to do. Of the twenty-seven kids now on death row, I think they all have a lawyer. Of the other two thousand adults on death row, a good number of them do not have an attorney and could go all the way to execution without one.

"The most serious problem is at the trial when they are appointed public defenders. The public defender, while he usually is a very competent attorney, has a big case load and not much experience in death penalty cases. I think they often don't do as good a job as you would have hoped they would do at the trial level. By the time they get to the appeal level, if the trial hasn't been conducted in all the right ways, then it's sort of hard to get relief on it.

"I think the real problem is the quality of representation they get at the trial level. I don't know if there is anything unusual about that for juveniles facing the death penalty because the adults who face the death penalty also do not get very good representation.

"It's often not because the attorney is not able, but because there is an enormous amount of pressure on the attorneys. They have a huge case load so they don't have the time to devote to it that they should, and there is a lot of political pressure in it. If you had an attorney in your hometown take a murder case representing somebody whom the press was hounding every day and the politicians were making speeches about, it's pretty tough to practice law in that community. You're going to hurt your law practice, you're going to make all your present clients angry, your kids are going to get shouted at at school.

"There's an enormous amount of difficulty for local attorneys to take local cases because they're sensationalized by the press and they make the attorney out to be some kind of monster and it's just very difficult to deal with. It's easier for someone from out of state to come in and do the job. They're not going to care if anyone in the town likes them or not. They can leave and go home and nobody knows what he's been doing or who he's been defending.

"If you have to live in the town and practice law there and see those people in church, and in the grocery store and everywhere else, then you'd get labeled as the guy who's trying to help that young murderer get off. The political pressures are really enormous for these attorneys and I really feel for them. They have to make a living and they have to live in that town so while I criticize the general level of representation these kids are getting, I have to understand the difficulties these attorneys are facing.

"We have fourteen states who have juveniles on death row at the present time. Only three of them have been executed since the death penalty has been reinstated. One was in South Carolina and the other two were in Texas. These were all seventeen-year-olds and they were executed in eighty-five and eighty-six.

"Charles Rumbaugh was born on June twenty-third, nineteen fifty-seven, one of several children in the west Texas white Catholic family of Harvey and Rebecca Rumbaugh. Raised in a constantly moving family with a violent, alcoholic father, Rumbaugh committed his first serious offense, breaking into a schoolhouse at age six. At seven he was wild and uncontrollable. At thirteen he was placed in the reform school. He spent the next four years there, fulfilling his ambition to learn how to commit more and better crimes. In Rumbaugh's own words, the Texas juvenile justice system 'took a thirteen-year-old troubled boy and turned out a hardened criminal.'

"Once released, he began his life of crime in earnest. Soon he was in a mental hospital for treatment of manic depression. He escaped from the hospital early in nineteen seventy-five and continued his life of crime. He decided to commit his next robbery of a small jewelry store. He pointed the gun at the jeweler and demanded the money but the jeweler resisted and reached for his gun. They struggled and Rumbaugh got the better of him. He shot twice and killed him.

"Police questioned Rumbaugh and he provided them with a written confession. He was tried and found guilty of murder and robbery and sentenced to death.

"Rumbaugh seemed resigned to his death sentence, writing in a letter that 'if they were to come to my cell and tell me I was going to be executed tomorrow, I would feel relieved, in a way. The waiting would be over. I would know what to expect. To me, the dying part is easy, it's the waiting and not knowing that's hard. I feel like I have been traveling down a long, dark and winding tunnel for the past nine years, the length of time I have been on death row, and now I can see no end to the tunnel, no light at the end of it, just more long years of the same. I have reached the point where I no longer really care.... I'm so damn tired and disgusted with sitting here and watching my friends take that final trip to the execution chamber, one after the other, while I continue to wait and speculate about when my time will come. They're killing me a little bit each day.'

"The day before his execution Rumbaugh was visited by friends he had corresponded with over the years and by three sisters and a brother-in-law. His mother went to the prison but at the last minute decided not to see him. Shortly after midnight, Rumbaugh faced his execution calmly. He refused communion and requested that no religious persons be with him at his death. He gave a last statement to the witnesses at his execution. 'About all I can say is goodbye. For the rest of you, even though you don't forgive me my transgressions, I forgive you for yours against me. That's all I wish to say. I'm ready to begin my journey.'

"He was the first person to die for a crime committed while under age eighteen in the post–Furman era of capital punishment. Was he deterred by the death penalty? 'I was seventeen years old when I committed the offense for which I was sentenced to die, and I didn't even start thinking and caring about my life until I was at least twenty.'

"Juveniles generally don't get treated as harshly as do the adults for almost anything they do. That's the reason we have juvenile courts to take care of them. There is a principle in our law that says juveniles can't commit horrible acts and do serious harm to people. They are not held fully accountable for what they do. So it's a fact that juvenile killers don't get as harsh a punishment as an adult killer. I think it's more of a surprise that some actually do get the death sentence, they're sort of the case that slipped through the cracks so to speak, or were treated strangely. I think it's fair to say that these are exceptional cases.

"They aren't the worst killings by any means, they aren't the worst kids, and they aren't necessarily in the same towns or the same states. It's just hard to explain these cases because they are so very rare. The death penalty for juveniles is pretty much disappearing like it did for Tennessee. Most states are passing minimum ages right in the death penalty laws and saying, no matter what, if you're under a certain age you can't get the death sentence.

"That's been going on since nineteen eighty and the states that want the death penalty say they don't want it for juveniles. Even in the states that didn't put the age in the death penalty laws, the judges and juries started not giving the death sentence to a juvenile. It used to be fifteen or twenty juveniles got death sentences a year and now it's only two or three.

"Even for the worst offenses by children, legal processes have been followed for more than a century that are markedly less harsh and punitive than those for similar offenses by adults. Attempts are made to protect children during the legal processes and to impose nonpunitive, treatment-oriented sanctions on them for their offenses. Retribution and deterrence, the age old justifications for adult criminal sanctions, have only recently made minor inroads into the practice of juvenile corrections. Even though juveniles, just like adults, sometimes commit horrible offenses and sometimes suffer horrible abuses, juvenile offenders and victims are legally, socially, and politically different.

"In this century the youngest person to be executed was fourteen, in South Carolina. His case has gotten a lot of attention because he was so very young. He was really just a little kid and was so small he didn't fit in the electric chair. They had to adjust the straps to make him fit and his feet still kind of dangled.

"Leaders in the legal, criminological, and social policy fields almost universally oppose the death penalty for juveniles. The prestigious American Law Institute excluded the death penalty for crimes committed while under age eighteen from its influential Model Penal Code, concluding that 'civilized societies will not tolerate the spectacle of execution of children. This position was also adopted by the National Commission on Reform of Criminal Law.

"In August of nineteen eighty-three the American Bar Association adopted as its formal policy a resolution stating that the Association 'opposes in principle the imposition of capital punishment upon any person for any offense committed while under the age of eighteen.' That was the first time in the history of the organization that it took a formal position on any aspect of capital punishment. The *Washington Post* endorsed the ABA's policy and urged it as a minimum requirement for jurisdictions having capital punishment.

"All European countries forbid the death penalty for crimes committed while under age eighteen. More than three-fourths of the nations of the world have set eighteen as the minimum age for the death penalty. The United Nations endorsed this position in nineteen seventy-six. Another indication of the present global attitude is the condemnation of the death penalty by Pope John Paul II, the first such position by any pope in history. Even in time of war, the Geneva Convention prohibits execution of civilians under age eighteen at the time of the offense.

"If the number of juveniles selected for death sentencing and possible execution is only a tiny portion of the number of juveniles who commit capital crimes, how are they selected? In an analysis of the cases of the eleven adults selected for execution from nineteen seventy-seven through nineteen eighty-three, the conclusion was that they were not unique and no rational basis could be discerned for their resulting in execution. Justice Brennan concluded that these adult executions were *not* 'selected on a basis that is neither arbitrary nor capricious, under any meaningful definition of those terms.' Extrapolating from these conclusions about adult executions, the inference seems much stronger in the matter of juvenile death sentences and executions. Their even rarer and more random pattern of occurrence leaves no alternative to the conclusion that they are most freakishly imposed. No rational selection process can be determined, and one is left to conclude that the basis of selection is arbitrary and capricious.

"Does the Eighth Amendment to the Constitution prohibit the death penalty for crimes commited while under age eighteen? The Supreme Court has avoided giving a direct answer to this question but has provided a general analytical framework from which answers may be derived. The foregoing analysis suggests that the most persuasive answer, given this general analytical framework, is yes—the death penalty for juveniles is cruel and unusual under the Eighth Amendment. This answer follows from a step-by-step consideration of the supporting arguments for the death penalty as they apply to adolescents. In this application, the force of these supporting arguments either disappears or in some cases suggests that the threat of the death penalty may become an attraction to death-defying adolescents. The line should be drawn at age eighteen, since that is by far the most common age for similar restrictions and limitations. This line should emanate from the Eighth Amendment and should be imposed by the Supreme Court.

"Indications of a trend seem to be appearing. More and more state legislatures, trial courts, and appellate courts are excluding juveniles from the death penalty. Specific provisions are appearing in statutes recently amended by legislatures. Trial courts, even when they are authorized to sentence juveniles to death, are very rarely doing so. Appellate courts are finding a variety of reasons to reduce the death penalties of juveniles without imposing a blanket prohibition on all such sentences. State law seems to be moving, however gradually, away from the death penalty for juveniles.

"While some persons have been executed for crimes committed when they were as young as age ten, most of the juvenile offenders were age sixteen or seventeen when they committed their crimes; the average age was just over sixteen years. The younger offenders, particularly those under age fourteen, were executed in greatest numbers before nineteen hundred. That is also true of the nine female juveniles executed. The last female juvenile execution was in nineteen twelve.

"In line with the historical pattern for all executions in this country, the Southern states predominate in juvenile executions, with sixty-five per cent of the total. Georgia is the leader, with forty-one juvenile executions.

Other leading states are North Carolina, Ohio, New York, Texas, and Virginia. Thirty-five states and the Federal government have executed juveniles for their crimes.

This summary of the characteristics of these executed children and their crimes raises more questions than it answers. But perhaps it will at least serve to refute the commonly held belief that the death penalty has always been reserved for our most hardened criminals, the middle-aged three-time losers. While they are often the ones executed, offenders of more tender years, down even to prepubescence, also have been killed lawfully, hanging from our gallows, restrained in our gas chambers, sitting in our electric chairs, and lying on our hospital gurneys.

If we discard the death sentence for juveniles, what can be done about violent juvenile crime? Many persons support the death penalty for juveniles from fear of and outrage over violent juvenile crime. This fear and outrage is shared by all reasonable persons, whether they are for or against the death penalty. Two answers to this problem suggest themselves. The temporary solution is to impose long-term prison sentences on such violent juveniles. That would ensure that they were reasonably mature adults and had been subjected to whatever rehabilitative programs were available before they were set free again. Life imprisonment without possibility of parole seems an unwise choice, like any personal or business decision that we vow never to reconsider regardless of future events. Few of the violent juveniles would be good candidates for parole in less than ten or twenty years, but that option should be left open for them to work toward.

"Unfortunately, no one yet has the cure for violent juvenile crime. It seems clear, however, that the death penalty for juveniles has been given a long trial period and has been found wanting. Its societal costs are enormous, and it delays our search for a rational and acceptable means of reducing violent juvenile crime."

Part II. The Men on Death Row

Eighteen

Richard Simon

Among other reasonings, who deserves the sentence of death is based upon the individual's ability to be rehabilitated. This aspect of the person who committed a capital offense is questioned by the courts. Can a murderer possibly reform, and can he make some contribution to society?

Most men on death row murder only once, contrary to the visions many of us have. Also contrary to popular opinion, some do have the ability to reform after their crime was committed.

Richard Simon was brought to Tennessee's death row when he was 20 years old. He has been on the row for almost nine years.

Richard was born in High Point, North Carolina, and was raised in Chicago. He was the youngest of three children and describes his family as "very loving." Tragedy struck early in Richard's life when his father died when Richard was five years old. His mother, a registered nurse, always taught him to take care of himself. He tried to live up to his mother's words and wanted to be the man of the house after his father's death.

Growing up in Chicago, Richard got into minor trouble along the line. Today he reflects: "My desire to be slick got me into a lot of trouble, but it was a way of life I chose. I cannot blame anyone but myself for the way I was then. I know and I believe I made a lot of bad choices in my life, and this started when I was a teenager."

Richard went to Tennessee by way of the Army. He joined the military to try to get out of street life in Chicago.

"I have never been married," he said. "When I was very young I got a girl pregnant but we were just too young to get married and raise the child. Then a couple of years later I was living with a young lady and we had two children. We were living as man and wife but I wouldn't commit myself to her completely. I'm paying the price for that now. I haven't seen or heard from them since I got into trouble. She did marry and has a life of her own now. I was a very selfish person and I'm only to blame for the wall I built around myself."

"I cannot really say when I made the choice to get involved in criminal activity," he says. "I think I led myself to believe that it was okay to do certain things. I sold dope and led the street life while in the Army. So I think I was two people—the person I thought I had to be and the person I really was. All the while I was doing wrong, I would go out of my way to do something good. I guess this was my way to rationalize my bad acts. Robbing a dope house was not like robbing a bank. And as one can imagine it got me into a lot of trouble. Not with the law so much, but with myself. I became a person who would do almost anything in chasing that almighty dollar. And before I knew it, I was in jail charged with murder."

Richard was convicted of murder during a robbery. His two codefendants received life sentences. At the time of his arrest, Richard claims that the authorities used illegal evidence to arrest him and also violated the codefendants' rights. Richard was appointed an attorney by the court, who probably never handled a capital case before. "You asked do I think I'm innocent of the crime that sent me to death row. Legally, yes, I am innocent. I believe I should never have been convicted of first degree murder. Second degree or maybe manslaughter. At the time of my arrest at age nineteen, I was very unfamiliar with the law."

"If I had one wish," says Richard, "I would want to let my mother know that all her suffering hasn't been in vain. And my being here isn't a reflection of her. Just let her know that I love her. And I know she is the best.

"Here I am a person who did things for a hobby now in jail with people who did things because they had to. And with me being in jail for taking someone's mother away with the way I love my mother really done a lot to me.

"I had always been in a hurry to grow up and I had to do it in jail. And had to do it fast. And with most black males charged with taking the life of a white woman I was sent to Tennessee's death row. I was only twenty years old and my life was all over. I couldn't believe this was real. I mean, death row was supposed to be for the real killers.

"Life on death row is strange as it comes. A person can lose sight of who he is, and if you don't know who you are to start with, a person really has a problem. My first years on death row I was lost. On the surface people thought I was okay, but on the inside I was a wreck.

"I did not find myself till after four years in this place. My true personality finally came to the top. I was no longer lazy. I was now eager to work hard at being a good person. It just came to me from within.

"I am not saying that I became perfect, but I did become conscious of my actions. Which means I quickly lost a lot of my bad habits. I started to care about others and myself, and when a person starts to care for others he is on his way to becoming a person worth saving.

"I have been sitting on death row all these years with my death hanging over my head. And I really would like to be a man before my death. I came to this place a very young boy, but it took a lot of sleepless nights to change. A person can lie to others, but he cannot lie to himself. And this is what I've stopped doing.

"Being on death row has been very painful for me and those who love me, but it has also been what has changed me. Sitting in a small cell with no comforts of home really is a lesson in life. There is no love behind these walls. Besides becoming closer to my family I have now come in contact with a lot of people who like me as a human being, and not just Richard — for whoever he may be. So even if I am to be killed in this place, at least I would have finally grown up. But I still do not want to die just yet. I have a lot of wrong to correct."

Richard has taken more of an interest in religion than he used to. "I never took the time to seek out a relationship with my God. But I have plenty of time. I also have a desire to learn now."

Since he's been on death row, Richard has taken an educational course on computers and a precollege course. He has given up on a college education now and is more interested in learning a trade.

Richard sees nothing of the outside world but for a scant hour or so of exercise outdoors per day. On Mondays, Wednesdays and Fridays he lifts weights. Tuesdays and Thursdays he usually joins in a short game of basketball. His in-cell time, which accounts for about 23 hours of his day, is spent reading, watching television, or just staring out in space.

It is difficult for Richard to think of the future for himself, as his future at the moment means only to die. "I couldn't honestly tell you my future plans if all this wouldn't have happened. Except for a job and family. Knowing what I know now, I wouldn't be involved in the street life." Richard is a father of three children, whom he hasn't seen since he's been on death row. "Another sad part of me being here," he adds.

"I believe that if I don't get any help soon, I might be executed. Because these people are playing for real. But I might get a life sentence somewhere down the line. So anything might happen. I have no idea. I just pray for a second chance. No one wants to spend his life or die in this place.

"I miss being free. I miss so much. I should be watching my kids grow up, and my mother grow old." Perhaps the most tragic result of capital punishment is that it is irreversible. There are no second chances once the punishment is carried out. A man, such as Richard Simon, may reform inwardly before he is put to death. But it may be too late.

Nineteen

Don Johnson

Don Johnson was born in Tipton County, Covington, Tennessee. He grew up in the fifties and sixties and says he didn't know how to reach out. "My parents didn't know how to reach me, and I had three sisters. We didn't get along very well either. I did a lot of things growing up and don't rightly know why. I wrote bad checks and ran away from home, stole things, and I guess it was to get recognition. I wanted to be noticed as I felt my family did not really know I was there unless I was doing something bad. I guess you could say I was abused as a child. My dad was very dominating and he used to beat me. Both my parents worked while I was growing up so we had enough food and things. We weren't really poor, I guess middle class. My mother and father still don't get along all the time, it's just a situation that many families have to deal with. I was sent to a reform school twice as a child.

"There were some happy times while I was growing up but not many. I used to spend the summers with my grandmother before she died and then I would stay with my aunt. I really enjoyed those days. There wasn't any really great times, and I remember when my mom and dad would go on vacation they would leave me with relatives and go off.

"I lived a life of crime but nothing violent. Writing checks was my worst habit back then. I moved to Ohio and for a while things went fine, then in nineteen seventy-two I pulled an armed robbery and did three years in jail for it. I was let out on early release and had my parole transferred to Georgia.

"I was living with a woman and her son and ended up marrying her. She was my third wife and after we were married, she changed considerably and it just wasn't working out. I sent her back to her parents and divorced her. Since that time I have had no other arrests other than the one I'm convicted of now. I decided that I didn't want to spend my life in prison and living the life of crime and figured I would go straight."

Don would work 60 or 70 hours a week to support himself and continued to do well. He tried to get into church, but found that the way some Christians were living was worse than things he had done so he gave up going to church.

Life went on and he met a girl named Connie. She had been married before and had a little girl. Connie was real young at the time they met and had been through a lot with her first marriage, having been beaten time and time again. They discovered they were in love and were married.

"We had a lot of problems the first year of our marriage," Don replied. "Most of it was because of difficulties she had endured during her first marriage. We couldn't seem to communicate and it was driving me crazy never knowing if she would be there or had taken off to be alone. We had been married for seven years and the last year had become closer than ever before. My son Jason was born in nineteen eighty-one and I was so proud that at last I had a son of my own.

"I would take the kids to the zoo when Jason was old enough and Connie and I got along real good the last year or so of our marriage. Of course we had our arguments the same as any married couple but on the whole, we had a good time. I had adopted her daughter Cindy a year after we were married and thought of her as my own.

"I always worked to take care of my family and made sure they had whatever they needed or wanted. Things I never got as a child that I wanted. I tried to make sure I didn't make the same mistakes I felt my father had made as I was growing up and tried to show my family the closeness that I felt a family should have.

Connie, Don's wife, was murdered on December 8, 1984, at a camping center that he managed. Her body was found at a shopping center several miles from the camping center.

"The man that murdered my wife was on work release. He worked for me and he came in and said that I committed the murder and that he helped me with it. He testified and lied on the stand but they used his testimony to convict me, which is all they had. They had to know he was lying for I could prove some of the things he said was lies. He wasn't charged with the crime or given immunity or anything. They just took his word and his testimony that I was guilty.

"When I was arrested, I was on the verge of suicide and didn't know what was going on in my life. I just couldn't believe what was going on and I decided that everyone was crazy. I gave up my religion as I felt they didn't care about anyone anyway. They wouldn't let me have a bond and my family knew I didn't murder my wife. My children were abducted by my sister-in-law the day I was arrested and I haven't been able to see or talk to them since then.

"I decided to end it all and it was in the jail in Memphis that I went to the chapel to pray. Everything in the service seemed as if it were hitting home to me and when he got through I found myself down front and got on my knees with him and said I wanted to give my life to God and I wanted to be a Christian. I asked him to help me and I got a feeling that I've never had before. This time the feeling didn't wear off and I asked God that I wanted Him to help me and show me the way. I felt like a new person.

"It was only through God that I've been able to get through this whole mess. I was convicted and my heart was in my throat when I heard the verdict. It was a very trying time and when I first walked into the death row cell it's hard to describe the feeling I had. The cell was empty and I had nothing but my Bible and bunk.

"After being on the row for a while I thought I would learn law so I would know how the attorneys had handled my case. I had to get my family to send money to buy books and I read everything that I could get my hands on. I found many things that had been wrong in my trial and hopefully I can get a new trial with the things I have found wrong.

"I have quite a few people involved in my case trying to help me out. I feel in some point and time that I will get a new trial somewhere down the line. My original attorneys were hired and I paid them a retainer but since my family couldn't come up with the rest of the money, they were assigned to represent me on appeal. I didn't have anyone to testify in my defense, the attorneys actually didn't put up a defense for me at all."

"I am now a Christian. I was saved in nineteen eighty-five when I was in the county jail waiting for my trial. I tell you there's nothing like it. I am trying to live a Christian life in here, and do the best I can with what I have. The Lord has brought me a long way and He's really blessed me in a lot of ways. I'm real thankful that He has helped me to change to a better person and while I sometimes slip, I am really trying to set an example of being a Christian."

Don doesn't get many visits except once a year from his parents and from a minister from Nashville who comes up once in awhile. Visits and letters are the only thing keeping those on death row from going crazy. It keeps them in contact with the outside world and shows that someone cares.

Twenty

Cecil Johnson

Discrimination against the poor in our society is well established. A defendant's poverty leads to inadequate legal representation at trial or on appeal and is a common factor among death row populations. Capital punishment is a privilege of the poor.

Cecil Johnson was born on August 29, 1956. He went to a small school in Mr. Pleasant, Tennessee, during his younger years. His family was poor and often Cecil found the other kids laughing at him because he didn't have nice clothing. He hated that, and would not participate in school activities. "I didn't have the support of my family or family life to be excited about football or baseball," he recalls. "My father would drink and get drunk. I loved my father but I didn't like his drinking.

"My parents broke up when I was little. My mother took the girls, and my younger brother and I were left with my father. He had a job in Nashville and would leave me and my brother alone all week long while he worked. Then he would come home for the weekends.

"My brother and I learned to be alone. I was about nine years old then. I learned to cook and do the laundry for us during the week. Sometimes we'd skip school and go fishing. I loved to fish more than anything else and it took my mind off the fact that we were all alone.

"I couldn't understand why my mother would leave us and take the girls with her. I guess I loved my mother and yet at the same time I was mad at her. It wasn't easy to try and be the man of the house during the week. Some days we would go hungry and only have something to eat once we got home from school. There was no mother to fix us breakfast or dinner and I learned to cook on my own.

"Finally my father met this woman and she started staying with us. But that didn't work, we couldn't seem to get along. That's how I started to stay in Nashville with my uncle. I was about ten and stayed there until

I was twelve years old. I liked my uncle and stayed in school. I wasn't on drugs or alcohol at that time."

Cecil got his first job when he was 13 years old and worked part time while going to school for about a year. When he was 15 he finally went out on his own. "I found an apartment with a couple of other guys and quit school. They talked me into selling marijuana and I made more money than I ever had seen before. I thought I had it made then as I was putting money in the bank. Everything seemed to be going all right for a while but soon I moved on."

Cecil next got a job in a diner and found a room to live in. Everything seemed to be going all right but he wasn't making much money. Then a month later he moved back home. He stayed with his father until he met some people from Georgia. They were involved in a new corporation. He moved to Atlanta and began working for these men, recruiting others. Finally he tired of that and went back to Nashville.

"A friend and I tried to get in the Army together. I made it but he didn't pass the test. I stayed in for a little while until one day I got drunk and was fighting with the officers. They kept me in confinement and gave me a choice of staying there or getting out. I chose to get out.

"When I came back home I didn't tell anyone that I had been kicked out of the service but they found out soon enough.

"It was about this time that I met a girl. We soon were together all the time and it wasn't long before I asked her to be my wife. Before we were married it seemed like everything went along so well, but after it was so different. We had our ups and downs and it wasn't long before we were fighting about anything and everything. She got pregnant and had a baby girl. We named her Deangela and she was the prettiest thing I had ever seen. I was crazy about my daughter. I remember the first time she called me 'daddy' and it brought tears to my eyes. I guess I'll never forget those words she said over and over that she loved her daddy. Maybe things would have been different if I had had a real home life with my parents still together. I never really trusted anyone in my growing up years. We split up after that and I really missed my daughter."

Cecil then went back to live with his father and was looking for work the day the police came and told his father that they were looking for him. Cecil went down to the station and was charged with murder during a robbery on July 5, 1980. He was convicted of killing three persons, including a 12-year-old boy and two men. The boy was the son of the store owner, Bob Bell, who testified at the trial and identified Cecil.

"I was tried and sentenced to death and have been on death row ever since. I didn't do the crime that I was convicted of," he says.

Tennessee's death row is a one-story brick building. Inside this meager structure are four walkways. Three have 13 one-man cells with walls on three sides and bars on the fourth. No cell faces another. The fourth row contains seven cells, two holding cells, and the death chamber where "Old Sparky" stands waiting with open arms. Each cell contains a man who waits to die.

"Since I've been in here, I've read the entire Bible. I feel closer to the Lord, closer than I've ever been. I read every day and find myself praying on a daily basis. It's something that I seem to do now. I find myself asking the Lord to give me strength to do what's right. I also pray for the people that don't like me. My biggest fear is not being able to be with my daughter and grandmother. I want to teach her some of the things that I've learned about life.

"I've come a long way since being here. I used to be selfish but now I've changed. I'm more considerate and I consider other people's feelings. I look at life in a better perspective and found in my heart I know what I want. That's to have a little peace. I don't need all the things I used to think I needed, the best clothes, best car, the best female. That's not important anymore.

"Sometimes I feel I just want to be alone because it seems to release a lot of my feelings. I feel like I've never really loved anyone. I haven't given up though. If my sentence was to be commuted tomorrow I would find my daughter and give her a big hug. That's something I missed in my life. I didn't have anyone to hug me if I was happy, sad or whatever."

Cecil feels that life could have been different if he had been raised with a mother and a father. Living together and creating a home.

"I seem stronger than I ever realized I'd be about myself. I find myself trusting people more, because I've learned that everybody's not the same. Even though everyone has their faults, their ups and downs, they are not the same. Just because you don't go to school doesn't mean you stop learning. I learn everyday, even here on death row.

"My mother and I have become closer now. I don't understand it, but it seems like I find myself trying to ease her pain that she's going through with me in here. She noticed the change in me too, and I feel that I can understand her better than I used to. I feel that she needs me now more than she ever needed me. I guess she needs me more as a friend, which is something all of us need sometimes. A person has to learn the things they need to learn so late in life. It's an odd feeling."

Cecil says he would like to do something that would help all the people that are sad. Because he knows what sadness is all about. He writes poems about his feelings and the pain and loneliness of living on death row. Mostly he sits in his cell writing or watching television. He doesn't get many visits but cherishes the ones that he does get.

Twenty-One

Billy Groseclose

Plea bargaining results in offenders whose crimes and circumstances are alike receiving widely differing sentences. Where there is more than one defendant in the same case, it is not unusual for one to be offered a lighter sentence for testifying against the others. Several men have been executed in situations where a codefendant, sometimes the trigger man himself, has gotten a life sentence for his testimony. Prosecutors will drop a case if a defendant agrees to plead guilty to a lesser charge, and the prospect of the death penalty may encourage such pleas.

Billy Groseclose was born in Saltville, Virginia, in January of 1948. He went to elementary school through the third grade in this small farming town. His mother worked in the office of the U.S. Gypsum mine. His parents had divorced shortly after he was born and Billy never did get to know his father. He died when Billy was 13.

Billy and his mother lived with his grandparents and cousin Doris on a small farm. It was there that Billy learned to live off the land and take care of the farm animals. He had a cow and a pony that he would ride and although Billy was only six years old, he learned a lot about farming from his grandfather. They were close and could be seen working the fields together during the days. He taught Billy to trade off working for things he needed such as food for the animals. He would go to another farmer and do some work in the fields for hay to feed the cow and pony and life was fun. He loved the farm life and the animals and the freedom to do as he pleased.

"I moved to Kingsport the year I was ten," Billy says. "I hated to leave the farm and the life I loved to live in the city. Although Kingsport is by no means a big city, I could not have the animals and the freedom to run the fields like I was used to doing.

"I had spent the summer living with my cousin and her husband and

75

when summer was over, my mother came to pick me up. She said she had been offered a better job in Kingsport and I would soon like it there as much as the farm. I knew I wouldn't ever like it as much but I had to live where my mother said. She would be a payroll clerk for the city so we all had to move there.

"I really tried to get along in school, but after having the run of the farm, I just didn't fit in and hated everything about it."

When Billy was 12, he got a job as a roller-skating carhop. He would work there every afternoon after school for his spending money. He didn't like working for anyone with all the rules and confinement it meant. People would throw trash and many times he would go flying through the air as his skates would tangle in the mess.

One day he had to take his skates to be fixed at the Skateland Center. There he was offered a job as skate boy. He would fix skates, sweep the floor, and clean the bathrooms. He was shown how to put the skates together. They all came in separate boxes and he would have to screw the parts together before anyone could skate with them.

"After two years there I became manager and I loved working at that place. My boss, Ray McCoy, was having trouble with the business slowing down, so I thought of giving free passes out to the kids at school. This idea went over real well and soon we were filled with kids skating. Business was picking up and we remodeled the place. It was looking good and I would come in many times alone to open up.

"I had worked there for four years when my boss decided that he had to sell the place. I tried to get a loan and buy it from him, but the bank would not loan money to me. Said I was too young to be owning my own business. It hurt a lot that I was going to lose out on having my own place, but I could not raise the money needed to buy it.

"It was about that time I enlisted in the Navy and went to the Great Lakes for basic training. I had joined the Navy as I figured I could swim longer than I could fly if I had joined the Air Force. I had a special girlfriend, Susan Lovin, and we decided to get married one day when I came home on leave. We just went out shopping and decided to go across the border into Canada and get married. We wouldn't tell anyone because in that time if you were married, they would not let you go to school."

Billy was stationed in Charleston, South Carolina, on the *USS Cone*. He took many courses during this time and got a degree in chemistry. He liked the Navy but missed having his wife with him. She had not told her parents that they were married, but had confided in a cousin.

"Susan called me one day to say that her cousin had gotten mad at her and told her parents that she had married me. Of course she had to quit school and we decided that she would move down here with me. That was much better anyway, I decided, and I found a small apartment. She could stay with me while I was in port, and move back with her family while I was out to sea. We were happy to be together and married life was wonderful. Life was going great with us and we had the world on a string.

"My time was up in nineteen sixty-nine and we went back to Kingsport to be with the family and decide what I would do next. I didn't want to reenlist but I wasn't sure what kind of work I wanted to do. For the next month we just visited with family and friends and had a good time."

Billy found a job at a car dealership in Kingsport and was sent to Rock Island, Illinois, to learn suspension and mechanic work. He also learned to fix transmissions and every part of a car. For two years he worked as a mechanic and life went on smoothly.

"My wife became pregnant and my son was born in nineteen seventy-one. I was so proud of him and loved my wife even more than I ever had before. I had signed up for the reserves and became a Navy recruiter. It was a full time job and we were sent to Memphis, Tennessee. My second son was born in April of nineteen seventy-three and we were the happiest of couples.

"Then I had to spend more and more time on the road, often being gone from home days at a time. My wife became lonely and started having an affair. It didn't take long for me to find out about it and when I confronted her with it, she admitted that she was in love with him. I told her I would forgive her if she would stay and work out our problems, but she was definite about leaving. I still loved her and I would miss the babies, but I let her leave. I could not hold someone that did not love me. She moved back to Kingsport and stayed with her family."

Billy met and fell in love with Debby in 1975. They were married and lived in Memphis for the next two years. Their lives were much like many others, with occasional fights that most married couples have. On the whole, Billy felt that their marriage was pretty normal. Then she was murdered and Billy was arrested for the crime.

Billy was tried for hiring two men to murder his wife. He says he never did that, he would never harm his wife or anyone else. The court believed otherwise and sentenced him to death.

Since being on the row, Billy has ministered to the other inmates there, many times stopping trouble before it begins. He has been called the "Death Row Preacher" by those who know him. For many inmates who have been angry or depressed, Billy has counseled them until they felt better knowing that someone cared.

Harmon Wray started visting Billy when he was first put on death row and has continued through the years to come once a week or every other week to visit in the small visiting room there in the death house. He says of Billy, "During the time that I've been seeing him, he has calmed a lot of people down and probably stopped a lot of violent situations from occurring."

"I realize there are only two choices in life," Billy says calmly. "You can either smile in a situation or you can cry. Most of the times you can't choose but when I can, I try to laugh. Living in this place is like being buried but not dead. It's like entombed, and there are few pleasures."

Being sent to death row made Billy start to look at himself and he turned to God. This led him to the ministry and he was ordained in the Church of God while there. He also does paintings of cartoon characters and sells them for pocket money to buy the necessities that the state does not provide, such as deodorant, toothpaste, powder, cigarettes and other items.

"Camaraderie on the row is strong. There's a solidarity back here, and when a guard comes back and yells at one guy, he doesn't realize he's yelling at all of us. I hope that one day I will get off death row for I don't like to think about Tennessee's final answer to justice, the electric chair."

Twenty-Two

Gary Cone

A popular argument for the death penalty is that capital punishment is a deterrent to crime. Potential killers will, supposedly, be frightened off by the idea of execution and will stop themselves from carrying out their plans.

People who commit a premeditated murder for the most part plan so carefully, they don't expect to get caught. They plan their escape, count on it, and don't consider their capture. The "death penalty" is probably taken, if at all, lightly.

Those who don't plan on committing a murder barely think about the murder itself, let alone the consequences. Most murders are the result of an impulsive act, with alcohol and drugs playing vital roles. The crime may happen so fast, and the person committing the act may be so highly intoxicated, it is hardly remembered by the killer himself. Such is the case with Gary Cone.

Gary Cone went to school just outside Fort Campbell, Kentucky. His father was in the Army and was stationed there for six years. He had an older brother, who died at the age of 15, and two sisters. The Cone family traveled from base to base, and Gary was moved from one school to another, always having to make different friends and begin anew. Their stay in Kentucky was one of the longest.

During his school years, Gary was far above his classmates. He was rarely absent from school. He liked it. His I.Q. was well above average, and he was referred to as "a genius" by those who were aware of his scholastic efforts.

Gary remembers his father as a harsh and unlikeable man. When his father was stationed overseas at times, Mrs. Cone would take her children to Lake Village in southeast Arkansas. She would more often than not make the children's clothes and, while they had plenty to eat, there never was much left over for some of the extra things in life.

In 1966 Gary graduated from high school and later joined the Army. After his basic training, he was sent to Germany. He then requested that he be sent to Vietnam. Gary first got his start taking drugs there, when they were given to him by the Army medics.

The horrors of war were too much for Gary to cope with. Women and young children were frequently befriended and subsequently caught hiding grenades in their clothing. It seemed as if you couldn't trust anyone and had to be constantly on the alert. The heat was frequently over 100 degrees, and the bugs bit day and night.

Gary rose to the rank of staff sergeant and earned a commendation. Taking body bags from the fields, some of which contained the bodies of his friends, was one of the many things in the line of duty he had to do. His visions in sleep were clouded by the sights of a buddy's head being blown off, and dying women and children he had seen left in the fields. These memories would remain with him for the rest of his life.

Gary started taking speed and opium. They were inexpensive, and it made life there easier to cope with. At times they felt like a necessities to him, such as when he pulled 53 straight nights of guard duty on the base perimeter and had to stay awake. After a year in Vietnam, he was honorably discharged and went home to go to college.

Gary majored in banking and finance and graduated in 1972. He did well enough on his law test to seriously consider going to law school. He continued taking drugs of various types, almost anything he could get. He found that he could not stop. It was a way of life to him.

In 1972 he met and fell in love with Glenda Cale, a student at the University of Arkansas. They soon became engaged.

Gary decided to attend law school at the University of Tulsa, with his GI bill paying the cost. Vietnam still stuck with Gary, and he found it difficult to talk about his problems with his friends. Glenda thought that he was dealing in drugs, as he always seemed to have money. He was, however, getting his money to support his drug habit from robberies of gas stations and convenience stores. Two months before he was to start school, he was arrested and sentenced to 25 years in an Oklahoma prison for armed robbery. Glenda and Gary broke off their engagement.

He hadn't been in prison long when his father died. Soon after, he learned that his girlfriend was raped and killed by an escapee from a Nebraska mental hospital. The world had stopped for Gary, and he took more drugs to erase the pain. Friends turned him on to heroin. He began to mainline. He couldn't find any reason to straighten out his life.

Prison life had changed Gary. He was bitter about his life and about the lost years he had spent incarcerated. He was always high and never wanted to come down. He never knew what was going on around him and barely knew what he was doing, and he didn't care.

Once paroled Gary tried to put his life in order. He was accepted in the Arkansas Law School. He wanted a career in law. Even though as a convicted felon he could not be admitted to the bar, he still wanted to pursue a career in the field.

Gary had a few months before school would begin, and he tried unsuccessfully to find work. There were no jobs that he could find with his record. He then turned to the trade that he knew: robbery.

He chose drug stores as he needed drugs as well as cash. He never wanted to hurt anyone. If something should happen to go wrong, he planned to just run away. He believed all of this would stop once he started school. He spent a few weeks in Hawaii, strung out on cocaine and losing touch with reality. Before the fall term began, he started his return to Arkansas.

On August 8, 1980, he robbed a grocery store. The next day he went into another store and filled a bag with over $100,000 worth of jewelry. He was seen leaving the parking lot and was soon chased by the police. They followed him at speeds over 60 miles an hour through residential areas. Gary finally abandoned his car and ran on foot, with the police fast behind him. Gunfire was exchanged, and an officer was wounded.

He eluded the police and spent the night in a burned-out building. Police closed in and fired tear gas into the structure, but Gary hid in the fireplace and they soon gave up. The long night of fear from the police, the shooting, and the tear gas brought his mind swiftly back to the jungles of Vietnam. It was over 100 degrees that day, and the sweat poured down into his eyes. He had not eaten in several days. He believed he actually was back in the war.

Gary broke in a house, entering from the back door. When he left the house that day, two people inside were dead. Gary does not remember killing them, but knows he must have. All he can remember is the police chasing, chasing, chasing him. He left the house and went to his sister's home. It wasn't long before he was arrested.

He stood trial and was given the death sentence. Today Gary Cone sits on Tennessee's death row.

Gary's elderly mother comes as often as she can to visit her son. You can see the pain and tears as she looks at him, wondering why it all happened. Gary looks back at her, also wondering why — and how.

The "deterrent to crime" theory does not hold with Gary Cone, or with many others who sit on the death row of Tennessee.

Twenty-Three

Mr. D

Racial discrimination was one of the grounds on which the Supreme Court relied in the *Furman* case in ruling the death penalty unconstitutional.

More than forty years ago, Gunnar Myrdal, reported that the South makes the widest application of the death penalty, and Negro criminals come in for much more than their share of the executions. In the past black offenders, as compared with whites, were executed for less serious crimes and for crimes less often receiving the death penalty. They were more often executed than whites without having their conviction reviewed by any higher court, whatever their age or offense.

Mr. D was born on September 2, 1934. He does not wish his name to be used in this book. "I was one of seven kids," he says. "We were so poor and I never did get an education. By the time I was fifteen, I was already getting into trouble."

Mr. D had three strikes against him: not only was he black, but he was also poor and uneducated. Society does not have any feelings for people unfortunate enough to grow up in this kind of atmosphere.

"The guy I am convicted of killing shot me three times before I fired at him. Yet my attorney did not give me a good defense. I had a court-appointed one who did not do his best to defend me." A majority of those in prison and on death row are the poor, young and minorities. That means that those who have few financial resources, or who are members of a racial or ethnic minority, will be more likely to die, while those who are well off can avail themselves of the legal talent to present their cases in as convincing a light as possible.

"When I look back on life and think about it, I wonder why those thirteen people can decide if I should die. My mother cries, every mother cries whose son is being sentenced to die. They hope that one day we will get off death row. Society does not feel our pain, the horror of knowing the exact hour and day that they will sit us in the chair and kill us.

"The years that I sat on death row, whenever I got a visit, they would not come and say, 'you have a visit.' They would yell 'get up! get ready!' I would sit in there shaking and nervous for there were always four or five guards out there. When I came out, they would chain me up like an animal and take me out to see my mother, father and my kids. We would only get twenty minutes to visit and if you were stupid enough to say anything about getting longer, you would be beaten once the visitors left.

"I lie in bed at night and wake up in a cold sweat. Tears running down my face and I'm scared. I'm just a walking dummy. I've already been killed, not in body but in spirit. When you sit on death row, you die three hundred sixty-five days a year. Each day it takes a lot out of us. The only time we get decent food is when some person is coming to check the prison out. Then we get good food and the public thinks we are well cared for. They don't want to know the truth.

"I've come close to being executed. I sat five doors from the electric chair. It was a hell of a life to live, knowing that someone was going to pull the switch sooner or later. Four hours before I was to die, a preacher came down and shook hands with me. He asked if my soul was right. I was in the holding cell that they have by the chair. They put you in there twenty-four hours before execution with nothing but your shorts and cloth shoes. This is so you cannot kill yourself and take the pleasure away from them.

"I had myself all ready to die, my head was shaved, but I didn't care anymore. I was crying but it was not tears for myself, but for my mother. For what I knew she was going through. All the other inmates were crying. Then I got a stay just an hour before time had run out.

"When I was taken off death row, the judge gave me ninety-nine years and said that I was not fit for society. But who is unfit? I remember the smell in the death chamber, the blood on the walls that I had to wash. The United States Supreme Court has ruled the death row here in Tennessee unconstitutional, but nothing is done about it. This has gone on for years and years. No one wants to hear the truth about the death sentence. They say we are animals and yet they do worse. Someone is paid to come in and pull the switch that runs electricity through our bodies and burn our skin off our bones.

"It wasn't long ago that a man, I won't say his name, killed his ex-wife and her boyfriend. He shot them both nine times. He had to reload over and over again to kill them. They said it was a crime of passion and he did not get the death sentence. He is a free man already. His father had the money to pay his way out of the crime. If I'd had money, then my crime would have been a crime of passion. I never should have gotten the death sentence but who out there cares. Every time there is an execution it is flashed on the news. It's only done for one thing, to make people hate, hate, hate.

"I remember sitting in my cell and they would bring in people to look us over. They would stand outside our cell and just stare at us like we were animals. If I would try to talk to them, they would cringe away like I would get through bars and try to kill them. I'm out in population now and off death row, but I'll always remember the horror of living there. Society wants to tear us apart. That piece of wood they call the electric chair is one of the worst, low down things that any man could sit another man in and kill him. I've been locked up for thirty-three years now and although I am only fifty-five, I feel and look like an old man."

Mr. D was working in unit six when he was attacked by a white inmate. He was stabbed five times with a six-inch, homemade knife. Guards made no attempt to break it up until Mr. D broke off a chair leg and began fighting for his life. He was transported to Baptist Hospital by Metro Fire Department thirty-six minutes after the stabbing. Reliable sources indicated that the conflict was over a personal matter and wasn't a racial one.

He doesn't know if or when he will ever get paroled. If paroled he doesn't know where he would go or what he would do. Society has said that he will never walk the streets again so he may well die inside the walls, his whole life spent behind bars. "I feel that God has forgiven me and I will be in heaven with Him no matter how society sees me."

Twenty-Four

Ron Harries

Ron Harries was born into a poverty stricken family on December 30, 1950. His mother Katherine was 17 years old and his father was in prison during most of her pregnancy. She finally moved to the city to live with her parents. She had to pay room and board and it wasn't long before she was pregnant again. Then she moved to the Valley View project and lived on welfare. She tried very hard to keep her family clean and fed but it wasn't easy.

Katherine's husband Bill came home from prison but it was not what she had expected. He began to beat her in front of Ron, who was only six years old at that time. Fortunately Bill was never home very much, but it was long enough to get Katherine pregnant again. Soon he was back in prison as she gave birth to two more children.

Ron never enjoyed the security of a stable home life. His father and uncles and most of the male role models were in and out of prison all of Ron's life. He would run away constantly to avoid the beatings, fightings, rapes and murders that he was constantly seeing at home and in the institutions. He spent two-thirds of his young life in institutions and it was a way of life to him. His grandmother and mother fought over Ron and he was placed first with one and then the other. His grandmother enrolled him in a Catholic school. He was teased constantly by the other children and often fought his way out of scrapes. His grandmother would then tie him to the bed and make him recite the rosary. He was told he was a bad kid over and over again.

Because he was passed around from place to place, Ron enjoyed no security. He saw himself as a bad boy that no one wanted. In the past 10 years of his life, he has managed to stay free 49 days. He was always high on drugs or alcohol. Ron first got into trouble at the age of nine and was placed in a boys' home. After that time he was in court more and more. His mother would come and get him in the beginning, then she would not come get him or would not show up in court when he got into trouble.

Since that time he lived in a string of boys' homes and halfway houses. When he was 16 in a boys' industrial school, he saw his best friend murdered right in front of his eyes. After that he just didn't care anymore and became solely interested in survival.

On August 13, 1963, he was sent to the Starr Commonwealth for Boys. It offered boys a home environment through its cottage-styled living. Twelve boys lived in one family with two house-parents. Each cottage family organized meals and activities. Ron began to like living there. He remembered loving his house-parents as he had never loved before. He said the two years at Starr Commonwealth were the best years of his life. He remembers only one visit from his mother in all that time. She had remarried, to a man named Blain. He was good to Ron only as long as he was sober, but he was usually drunk.

Ron was 14 when he ended up at the Hudson Farm. Only those who had been in several lesser security institutions ended up there. Most of the boys were older and they taught Ron well. They fought with chains and pipes, and rapes were frequent. They taught him how to use drugs and break into places.

Ron had lived a lifetime in his early years, never knowing love or family living. He went into the Marines, going to boot camp in 1968. While in the Marines he received a good clerical job in the P.X. He got his G.E.D. Unfortunately, the moment he stepped out of this controlled environment he was in trouble again. He went to see his grandmother who said he was evil and just a bum. With all doors closed, he returned to his mother and she took him in.

Ron was married to Sue in 1971 and they had a daughter. He tried to go straight and get a job. He made a down payment on a suburban house and bought new furniture. They moved in but Ron was jealous and would not let Sue leave the house without him. Things began to go downhill when his father was released from prison. Ron wanted to impress him and they drank together and did scams. It wasn't long before Ron came home and found the house empty. Sue had left him with nothing.

He started to look for his family and it was only after beating up his father that he was told where they were located. He went to Ohio to find them. He was high on drugs, committing robbery after robbery. He took a hostage in a robbery attempt and after holding her for a couple of hours, he let her go unharmed. The police picked him up and the charges included armed robbery, kidnapping, and possession of a firearm while commiting a felony. He received a sentence of six to twenty years.

Ron spent six years in prison. He was transferred to the prison in Lucasville, Ohio. This was the most secure prison in the state. It held all security risk prisoners. He spent his time and when he finally was released he had a drug habit, and an institutionalized mind held him captive.

Ron and his friend headed for Kingsport, Tennessee. They planned to pull three or four robberies and then head for Florida. It was January 22, 1981, that Ron went into the Jiffy Market in Kingsport, Tennessee. He needed money for his drug habit. "I was high on drugs at the time — all I wanted was the money and I won't lie about that. During the course of that somebody tried to thwart the robbery. It happened to be the clerk's boyfriend or fiancé or something. He screamed at me and ran at me. The gun was pointed at her and it went off." Her cousin came over and Ron made her give him the cash. He could have killed her but left without harming her. For this crime he was given the death sentence.

In June of 1984, Ron gave up his appeals. He maintains that he is ready to die in order to shock the public into seeing the gruesome reality of the death sentence. Having to stay in a solitary cell, cut off from normal communication from others, is a depressing experience that not many people can cope with. They are hated and feared by others and their lives have no meaning. "I've made my peace with God, but it took a long time," he said. Federal Judge John Nixon cancelled Ron's execution pending a hearing on whether drugs that had been given to him impaired his reasoning.

Harries' mother and four brothers had just completed their final visit with him. They were going to return to Cleveland, Ohio, to await news of his scheduled execution.

"My mother sat here crying on her last visit," Ron said. "She was crying not only for me, but for Rhonda Greene." He doesn't expect Rhonda's family to ever forgive him but he asks that they at least give him the opportunity to tell them he's sorry. "If killing my son would bring back Rhonda, I would find some meaning to Ron's death and I would accept that," Ron's mother said, but she was unable to understand a "revenge" killing.

"I made the ultimate mistake, but don't use the Bible with an eye for an eye — just say you're mad, you hate me for what I've done to your family — but don't say it's God's will," Ron said. "I killed somebody and there's no way that I can make amends for that and there is no way that I can condone it or make excuses for it — but I didn't torture Rhonda Greene. I know I was guilty, but it was not intentional or premeditated." In one conversation Ron told a friend that he has never had a single happy day in his life. He wonders why he shot Rhonda when other armed robberies ended with no one hurt. He cannot escape the memories that haunt him at night. His own daughter has the same name as the girl he killed.

Governor Alexander refused to commute his death sentence. Letters poured in from all over the world asking that Harries not be executed. One such letter said, "Stop executions in Tennessee, in the USA and all over the world. Reprieve Ronald Harries that you yourself get not involved in murder. The fact that the death penalty is abolished in the Federal Republic of Germany by the fundamental law says that the death penalty is unworthy of a nation like the United States. In our meaning, the death penalty is deeply cruel — and violates the dignity of human beings."

Judge Nixon stayed the execution days before it was scheduled. A next-friend suit was filed by friends of Ron's who feel that he was not of sane mind when he gave up his appeals. Attorneys said conditions on death row made Ron unable to make rational decisions.

Ron spoke of the conditions on the row. "It's filthy and dirty in our cells. Our showers are cut at eight minutes. We have to wear hot, unsanitary orange jumpsuits all the time. When prisoners ask for toilet paper, they are asked by guards if they think this is the Holiday Inn. I had ear surgery and my ear started bleeding. I didn't have medical attention for more than twenty-six hours."

"Death row is isolation that you can't understand unless you live it. Everyday is the same. You come out for a shower and if the weather is nice enough, you get to go outside for one hour. The exercise yard is small cages that have wire mesh even on the top so the sun cannot shine. All I have to offer is to write down things I feel because I hope somebody will say this will keep someone from doing the same thing I did. I lay back and wonder how I'll act when it comes down. Will I scream and holler on my way over there or will I be manly. I go to bed at night and hear the noises around me. Some radios playing, some televisions, and some snifflin'. Then I wonder if I'll be here a year or will I be dead."

When asked if he was ready to die, Ron said, "It's not so much being ready, I've accepted it. I think God has forgiven me for what happened. My relatives are upset, they cry when they talk to me. They want me to change my mind and resume my appeals. The state has had control over my life all the years I was locked up. I don't want them to have control over my death.

"I'm trying to make it harder for other death row inmates to be electrocuted. The point is that the inhumanness of the death penalty has to be brought out. One thing people are doing now is talking about the death penalty. That's good, that's positive."

Judge Nixon ruled that Ron was incompetent to decide his fate. Nixon based his ruling on testimony of psychiatrists who after examining Ron said he was not competent to make a decision while living in inhumane conditions on death row. Nixon also ruled that the "next-friend" petitioners who intervened on Harries' behalf when he dropped his appeals have standing and can appeal the inmate's conviction.

The stay of execution will remain in effect until disposition of the petitioners' lawsuit against the state, in which they challenge the constitutionality of the death penalty — with or without Harries.

Twenty-Five

Kenneth O'Guinn

Kenneth O'Guinn was born in Madison County, near Jackson, Tennessee. "I had four sisters and three brothers," he says. His father ran a meat packing company while he was growing up. They didn't have very much but there was always food on the table and clothes for all of them. "I was never what you call close to any of my brothers and sisters," he recalls. "My father made me leave home when I was only fourteen years old. I think it was because he drank all the time and didn't really know what he did a lot of the time. I felt bad and hurt because he threw me out but I didn't hate him. I didn't love him either, he was just my father. Things were never the same for Dad and me after this happened.

"I was scared at being on my own, but not really worried. I was big for my age and I knew if I got a job and a place to stay that I could make it. It was at that time that I joined a carnival. My mother came and signed a paper that I could travel with them. I loved her very much and she would always help me when I needed it. She was always there for me when I needed her and still is. She was the one who helped me with my school work, learning about Christ, my manners and other things. Since being here on death row, she has helped me to get a few of the things I can have.

"It was during this time that I met my wife. We dated for a while and then got married. Since I worked for the carnival I didn't have much time to date. We were both young and wanted to be together. Jan was a beautiful woman and deserved better than I could give her at the time we were married. Jan got a job with the carnival selling tickets for the rides. I worked operating them. It wasn't easy. We didn't make much money but we furnished a small house trailer. For six years we stayed married and had three kids.

"The first child was a girl named Cynthia, then we had a boy named

90

Kenneth, Jr., then the last child was a girl called Sonia. When Cynthia was old enough to start school, Jan decided to take the kids and go home." Kenneth finished the season out and then went home.

During the next year and a half Kenneth worked two jobs to make ends meet. He didn't have time to even be with his family and again decided to go back to the carnival to work. Jan didn't like his being gone for ten months a year and told him that if he didn't stay home, she would divorce him. She got the divorce a couple of months after that.

"From nineteen seventy-one until nineteen seventy-seven we tried three times to get back together and make our marriage work but it wasn't any use. We remained friends and decided to try again in nineteen eighty-three. This is when the Huntsville authorities arrested me on the murder charge. It was this charge I was later cleared of."

The authorities in Huntsville, Alabama, contacted Tennessee to see if there were any charges on Kenneth. They had a murder that was similar to the Alabama one. They sent a couple of officers down to question him about the murder. About three weeks later he was charged.

Kenneth was appointed an attorney who came to the jail to question him. The next time that Kenneth was to see his attorney was at the trial. The trial started late one afternoon and was over the next morning. There were no witnesses called for his defense and when he asked to be allowed to take the stand in his own defense, his attorney refused to let him. He was convicted of killing Sheila Cupples, a 17-year-old girl whom he had met at the Jackson tavern, and was given the death sentence.

It was hard for Kenneth to accept the death sentence. "I felt that the attorney that was appointed did very little in defending me. If I had the money to pay an attorney I'm sure that I would not have gotten the death sentence." It is often true that the poor and minorities who are unable to afford the skilled legal counsel are the ones who receive the death sentence. The arbitrary nature of capital punishment in the United States is significant for several reasons. It raises questions about the fairness of the judicial system. The issue of arbitrariness was precisely the issue cited by the United States Supreme Court in 1972 when it declared capital punishment unconstitutional.

Justice Byron White held that the death penalty constituted cruel and unusual punishment because "there was no meaningful basis for distinguishing the few cases in which it is imposed from the many in which it is not." The same crime committed in two different cities will draw two different sentences. Michael DeSalle said, "During my experience as governor of Ohio, I found that the men on death row had one thing in common: they were penniless—the fact that they had no money was a principal factor in their being condemned to death."

"The hardest part of the trial was seeing my mother," said Kenneth O'Guinn. "She had to hear the judge give me the sentence. I wish I could have spared her the pain that she was feeling at that moment. My wife and kids lived in Alabama and weren't at the trial.

"My mother was devastated and fell apart. She couldn't believe what the judge said when he gave the verdict and sentenced me. I pretty well knew what the sentence was going to be as my attorney had told me in the jail before the trial started, that he couldn't win my case. I'm still very bitter about the whole thing.

"Since coming to the row, I can see what hell is like. We have poor ventilation and the heating doesn't work. In the summer you are so hot it's hard to breathe. In the winter you can't get warm. We receive cold food because it sits out in the lobby until the guards feel ready to bring it into the part where we are located.

"The medical treatment is almost nonexistent. In order to be seen by a doctor you have to be on sick call that morning. If you become sick later on, they put you on call for the next day. Then you will most likely not see a doctor, but a nurse who will give you aspirin and tell you to go back to your cell. Some of the staff have said why should they treat us for we are going to die anyway."

Kenneth's mother sends him stamps and money when she can. She also comes to visit once a year. She can only come that one time as she has no way to get to Tennessee except with her brother. He brings her on his vacation. She has faith and the belief that something will happen to help Kenneth out of that place. She tells Kenneth to pray, read his Bible, and have faith that God will look over and take care of him.

"It gets lonely in here with nothing to do all day. We are only allowed to go outside of the cells for one hour a day. We are put in cages outside to get some air. All of the inmates are level one, two, three or four. If you are level one, you get to go outside with more than one person, if you are level two, you can be out with a couple of people. Level three and four must go outside by themselves. The rest of the time is spent in reading, watching TV, and just laying on my bunk. I did get my G.E.D. since being incarcerated.

"If not for the Reconciliation House, my family wouldn't even be able to visit once a year. Reconciliation House is where the families can stay overnight free of charge. It is for people who have someone in prison. They have to fix their own food and leave the room the way it was when they arrived.

"Jan writes to me every week and once in a while the kids do too. She is not able to come up to visit with me but is going to try to this summer. This would mean so much to me."

When asked if he thought that he would be executed, he replied, "I don't believe that I will be executed. I feel that they will overturn my sentence. I don't believe in the death penalty and never have. I don't know if I will be able to accomplish anything before my execution date, but I would like to see my kids and granddaughter. I was appointed a new attorney last January. But so far, I have only talked to him twice on the telephone. I've received one letter from him to inform me that he was now my new attorney. I think that I've about given up hope. I hope one day to have my sentence changed to life in prison so I can get off this awful place."

The decision to spare some murderers and execute others frequently hinges on factors that are beyond a criminal's control and are irrelevant to his guilt. Race, geography, the inclinations of the prosecutor, the talents of the defense attorney, and simple luck play important roles in what amounts to a lottery of death. New Orleans district attorney Harry Connick once said, "But that's what we have. One guy can get the death penalty while the guy next door doesn't for the same thing."

Twenty-Six

Byron Parker

Byron was the youngest of three brothers and two sisters in a middle class home. His parents, who recently celebrated their 47th wedding anniversary, raised their children with the utmost love and kindness.

"There is nearly forty years separating my parents and me," Byron says, "but never once was this age difference a result of any love being lost between us. My father, who retired from his job after thirty-five years, never made a lot of money but always managed to provide a roof over our heads, clothes on our backs, and food on the table. My mother, a full time housewife, saw to it that we were richly blessed with the things money couldn't buy. She supplied the love and patience equivalent to a pot of gold.

"My sister Teresa was like a mother figure to me since the age difference was so great between my parents and me, plus, Teresa could never have children so she sort of took me under her wing. I can recall waking up in the emergency room at the hospital after a severe car accident and the first faces I saw was that of Mom and Teresa. Any time I needed strength, I had Teresa. Any time I needed love, I had Mom. When I was married in New Mexico, it was Mom and Teresa who flew out even though they didn't have the money.

"If you notice, Dad wasn't the first one at the hospital for me all those times, nor was he at my wedding. Why? Because he was either working, or in bed getting ready for a new day's work. He was the one keeping the roof over our heads, heat in our home, food on our table, and clothes on our backs. Regardless of what he wanted to be when he grew up, I'm just glad he grew up to be my dad, because I wouldn't trade him for any other dad in the world.

"At age twenty-one, I began traveling the country as a direct marketing salesperson. I had worked at various other jobs before this

94

one, but only for long enough to earn gas and party money. It wasn't that I was irresponsible with the many jobs I had, I just felt that I was the all–American kid living the all–American teenage life. I dropped out of school in the eighth grade. I knew it all. I didn't need education, nor did I need a full time job. Why? Because I had friends, tons of them. And I had Mom to run home to when I needed clothes washed and good cooking. And then I had Dad to bum ten bucks from when I needed gas money. And I had my friends to remind me that, 'Man, this is life!'

"It wasn't until I became a husband and father that I realized what a fool I had been all those years. And it wasn't until I was sent here to prison that I realized the only 'real friends' I had were my mother and dad. They were the only ones who truly cared. It didn't take long to see that all the friends who proclaimed, 'I'll go to hell with you,' obviously weren't considering prison to be part of hell. I've been here for four years and I have yet to see or hear from any of them."

Byron left his hometown of Mableton, Georgia, in 1981 and began his job as sales representative. It was while traveling that he met Paula Mathers in Lakeland, Florida. She had joined the company and Byron walked into the office and saw her. They had a short courtship and were married six months later in New Mexico. The wedding was held at the Ambassabor Inn and about thirty of their coworkers attended.

"However," Byron continued, "the beautiful night was shattered, and I alone am to blame. I had been drinking all evening and by the time the reception had ended, I was plastered. I became a rude and crude person and wound up turning the night that was supposed to be the happiest of my wife's life, into a disaster. That night was nearly seven years ago, and my head is still hung in shame for my drunkenness that night.

"Our work carried us through every major city of every state across the U.S., and we would spend about two weeks in each of these cities. Paula and I were like two children after the working day ended. We explored the beaches in Florida under a star-scattered sky, we broused the gift shops of Charleston, South Carolina, and we found heaven in the mountains of Asheville, North Carolina. We once flew a jet out of Ohio merely because Paula wanted to meet my parents.

After a brief honeymoon in Colorado Springs, Colorado, they returned to Paula's hometown of Lakeland. During the following year, they both taught Sunday school classes and at the same time were blessed with the birth of a son, Byron, Jr.

"I guess I would be lying if I said life was going to be perfect for the three of us," Byron said. "In fact, life was dealing our little family some cruel hands, but we were happy and there was love in our humble little home.

"In September of nineteen eighty-two, the three of us moved up to Georgia where I had been raised. With Paula and I both working, we quickly settled in and found a nearby day-care center for our son. On weekends I played guitar in a gospel band. We would raise money for needy families and children needing operations. I can't explain the feeling I had as I played onstage knowing that our time there would help someone in need. It was truly an experience that I'll never forget. Not one penny went into our pockets for the many hours we spent playing, but I did receive an abundance of satisfaction and pride, and that's something money could never have bought.

"I was arrested for two counts of terroristic threats. This came as a total shock to everyone who knew me because they knew the good family I had grown up in. It was my sister who came to me and asked if I needed to talk to a psychiatrist. I told her that I did, I couldn't talk to anyone else, and thought a stranger would be better. I was about to explode, I was a walking time bomb and no one in the world knew it but me. I didn't know exactly what my problem was at the time, but I knew I had one boiling inside of me and it needed releasing. Perhaps I had watched too much television, but I assumed that all I had to do was walk in and see the shrink, spill my guts to her concerning things I swore I would never tell, and she'd make me all better.

"The first few visits I was just filling out papers and she never got around to asking me what was wrong. I had spent hours preparing myself with the courage to tell her things that was in my mind, but she would not listen to me. The only person that I had to talk to, that could help me, would not listen to my silent screams.

"On June the sixth, nineteen eighty-four, my whole world abruptly fell apart. I was arrested one week before my son's second birthday and charged with rape and murder. The crime that I am accused of committing happened during a twenty-minute time span that I was away from home, and occurred nearly ten miles away. Needless to say, I went to trial that November and was sentenced to die."

Sometimes Byron Parker speaks as if in a reverie. "As I sat in silence, I could still hear the sharp 'rap' of the judge's gavel. The sound echoed in my ears as I sat motionless upon the narrow bunk. Momentarily, my attention wandered to the three dismal gray walls surrounding me. My floor and ceiling were smooth concrete. Yet the wall cried out in compressed agony. Etched into these paint-splattered walls were the silent screams of those who had suffered here before me.

"I could smell the musty odors from the rotting souls of men who had endured the same small cell for many years before I even knew what 'breaking the law' meant. I could feel the cold air from my cellar-like new home seep into my bones, bringing with it the stagnant poison of failed dreams and lives lost to caged time.

"I slowly pulled the state-issued wool blanket over my trembling legs, clad only in the thin, white trousers, as I rested my head against the hard wall. My soul began to ache. My burning eyes slowly closed as I began to pay the price that losers often pay. Trapped by my own stupidity, the empty loneliness reached out to claim me."

Byron resumes his story. "Within two weeks of my sentencing, I was transferred here to death row in Jackson, Georgia. My first appeal to the Supreme Court resulted in the reversal of the rape charge against me, but the murder conviction and death sentence was upheld.

"In February, nineteen eighty-five, my wife and I were divorced. Due to my drinking and infidelity, I was slowly driving her away. It wasn't that I didn't love her . . . I did. But I had a secret problem that no one knew of but me. I would get drunk and when I got drunk I would cheat, and when I came home, the guilt would slap me in the face because there would sit my beautiful wife and son. Then I'd blame my drunken, cheating ways on her to ease my guilt. I have to hand it to Paula though, for she stood by me during my trial. I had put her through two years of drinking and cheating and still she stood by me until the very end.

"My friends have deserted me and my world has been reduced to a small eight by ten foot steel and concrete cell. I have been sentenced to die by a state whose motto is, 'We kill people who kill people to show that killing people is wrong.' I have had nine friends executed since I've been here, and three of them were my neighbors. As each of them were murdered, a small part of me died as well. Each morning when I awake and see these grey painted bars before me, I die a little inside. Each time I think of holding my son whom I haven't seen in three years, I die inside.

"My older brother Dean, who is a paraplegic, tried to break me out of prison. Not because he was mean or evil, but because he loved his little brother and could not live with the fact that I had been sentenced to die. He felt he had to do something and as a result he ended up in prison.

"There are four cell blocks in all, each one holding thirty living, breathing, human beings. We have feeling, we hurt, we cry, and we know happy and sad. But if we reach out for a want, need, or desire, our hands are slapped. We are screamed at, humiliated, starved and condemned."

Byron, like his brothers and sisters occupying the death rows across the country, has refused to give up. He clings to the hope that one day an end will be put to this senseless, premeditated murdering of those who

made a tragic mistake in life. He has spent the past years getting his
G.E.D. and taking many college courses. He had a book of poetry
published. He is also working on a novel he hopes to have finished in the
near future.

"There isn't a day that I don't stare through the dirt-stained window
across from my cell and wonder if I'll ever touch the trees and flowers
that I can see beyond. I wonder if I'll ever feel a mountain stream rush
over my feet, or see a sun rise or set beyond these walls. Or will I be
murdered here?

"The years drag by—life or death? I no longer know. Perhaps
both—perhaps neither. Painful thoughts flow into lost memories. Is this
life at which I'm gazing? Or just a hopeless stretch of time?"

Here is one of Byron Parker's poems:

"How to Love"

Mother taught me
How to crawl
How to talk
And how to stand
Daddy taught me
How to walk
How to run
And be a man

Twenty-Seven

Fred Coffee, Jr.

Fred Coffee was born in Washington County, Virginia, on March 20, 1945. His father was in the Army at the time and was stationed in Europe. For most of Fred's younger years, his father was never around. His mother had to raise his two sisters and younger brother all by herself. She would work two jobs sometimes just to make sure her children had decent food and clothing for school.

"Mom and Dad divorced in nineteen fifty-six, and we kids lived with Mom. My Dad remarried a woman with three daughters, and from time to time my brother, sisters and I would go and stay with him during the summer vacations.

"My brother and I were living with Dad in Wilmington, North Carolina, when I turned seventeen in nineteen sixty-two. I wanted to join the Navy but my Dad wouldn't hear anything of it. One day while he was away, I packed a few belongings and hitchhiked back to my mother's home in Bristol, Virginia. She signed for me to join the Navy, where I remained until nineteen seventy-four.

"While in the Navy, I served with the Navy's Seal team in Vietnam. The death and destruction I witnessed there haunts me to this day. I left the Navy in nineteen seventy-four and went from job to job, never really being satisfied with being at any one place very long."

Between 1964 and 1980, Fred was married and divorced three times. He has a daughter from his first marriage whom he hasn't seen since 1969. The other marriages produced no children, although he did adopt two boys that were his third wife's children.

"In nineteen eighty-six, I decided to move back to the old hometown and settle down there close to my mother and sisters. It was during this time I was questioned about and later arrested for the murder of a ten-year-old girl. She was supposedly killed in nineteen seventy-nine.

"My time spent in the county jail awaiting trial was pure hell due to a young child being involved. I was beaten twice by inmates and harassed by jail deputies. The pressure of it all finally got to me and I attempted suicide. Fortunately, fellow inmates in nearby cells alerted the jail staff and they cut me down. It was shortly after that in the dirty little jail that I found Jesus Christ. I had no one else to turn to. My mother wanted to help me but couldn't. Mom's a fine lady and has stuck with me through thick and thin, no finer lady ever lived. I went to trial in nineteen eighty-seven, and was given the death sentence.

"It was during my trial that I learned why my Mom and Dad had been divorced. Mom had been called as a witness during my sentencing hearing and said that my Dad had molested my sisters many times over several years. When she found out about it, she divorced him. He had also molested me during my younger years but I had only told my sister about it.

"During my trial, evidence was uncovered that another man was questioned and almost charged for the murder I was convicted for. The man himself admitted that he may have killed the little girl but couldn't remember. We were not allowed to present this evidence to the jury. If we had been, I'm quite sure the outcome of the trial would have been different. Witness after witness came forward in nineteen seventy-nine with information about the person they had seen the little girl with the day of the murder. A composite of the suspect and his vehicle was given coverage in the news media. Time after time the witnesses gave descriptions of the man being well over six feet tall with brown hair and driving a medium blue Ford van.

"At the time of the little girl's death, I was driving a solid white Dodge trans-van minihome. I am five foot seven inches tall and my hair is almost gray. Three eyewitnesses that saw the blue van, in a letter to the district attorney, and my attorneys, said they would testify in court that it was not my van they saw where the girl's body was found.

"This letter was not allowed to be put into evidence or read to the jury. After being told by the district attorney, all three testified it could have been my van and they may have been mistaken about the color. One witness still maintained it was a Ford van he saw."

There was a total of eight eyewitnesses against Fred. All but one testified that they had seen his picture on television and in the newspaper several times before they picked his photo out of a photographic lineup. All but three of the witnesses were nine to eleven years old. One eyewitness was excused by the trial judge because he admitted that he came to identify Fred because of the reward money offered. He was a close friend of the other eyewitnesses.

The district attorney argued that Fred's traumatic childhood and his experiences at killing children in Vietnam drove him over the line. The D.A. maintained that Fred had then killed a young girl out of frustration and to satisfy his sexual perversions.

"It's extremely difficult to accept my conviction and death sentence. Right up until the guilty verdict was announced, my attorneys and I were confident of a not guilty verdict. We were shocked when the verdict was announced. One of my attorneys wept. Although both attorneys were court appointed, I do believe they did their best in my defense. I was tried, convicted, and sentenced before my jury was chosen. I, like so many others, was tried in the news media.

"I used to be a believer in our judicial system until I became a victim of it. We are only pawns in our legal chess game, to be sacrificed if need be to further the ambitions of prosecutors.

"The most difficult part of my trial was seeing my dear mother sit back and see her son sentenced to die for the crime of someone else. Mom's never been the same since. She's been hospitalized twice and almost died. By the grace of God she's alive, and we continue to fight.

"Death row here in North Carolina, from what I understand, is better than most. We are not confined to our cells but have access to the entire block. We are not mistreated and we are well fed. We have access to the library and canteen and have religious services. There is so much hatred on death row. You cannot allow yourself to trust anyone. Racial prejudice is rampant. But one day, by the grace of God, I'll leave this place, but I will come back. Not as an inmate, but as one who cares for those who have become victims of our unjust justice system."

Twenty-Eight

Jeff Dicks

Jeff was born in Concord, New Hampshire, on December 6, 1957. He was the oldest of four children in a close-knit family. While they weren't rich by any means, the kids had everything they wanted and plenty of love. When Jeff was ten years old his family moved to Asheville, North Carolina, to live away from the cold winters up north. Being a close family, his grandparents soon moved South also. Then it was only a matter of time before the rest of the family, aunts and uncles and their families all moved to the Asheville area. There life was normal with weekend barbeques spent together with the family.

When Jeff was 15 he went to work selling Fuller Brush products with his mother. They would work together trying to see who could sell the most in the three hour time limit they set for themselves. Most of the time Jeff came out the winner for he had a charming way about him that people liked and trusted. Most of the money he earned he would give to his mother to help with the kids and paying rent on the new home they had moved into. Jeff's father was a mechanic and did not earn much money so they all had to work to get by. Life was going along well and they were all happy. He had two sisters and a brother who tagged along whenever they could.

By the time Jeff was 18 he met and fell in love for the first time with a girl named Betty. She was a year younger than Jeff and wanted to get married. They had a small wedding with just the family present and found an apartment. A couple of months later Betty found out she was pregnant. She wasn't happy for she had been in raised in an orphanage and didn't want to be a parent. She felt she was too young but Jeff was happy at the thought of being a father, for he loved children. He and Betty moved to Kingsport, Tennessee, and Jeff continued working for the Fuller Brush Company.

While in Tennessee Jeff had befriended a boy named Donald Strouth. He felt sorry for him and let him stay at his apartment until he could find work. Strouth would just hang around day after day not bothering to look for work but Jeff was too soft-hearted to tell him that he would have to move.

One day Donald Strouth, who everyone called Chief, and Jeff went out riding. Jeff was driving and Chief told him to pull over in front of a used clothing store just around the corner from Jeff's apartment. Jeff did as he was told and when Chief said he was going to rip the store off, Jeff just laughed, sure that he was only fooling with him. Chief went inside the store and when he came out a few minutes later Jeff saw blood on his jeans. Chief's hands were full of clothing and he dumped them in the back seat.

"I asked Chief what he had done in there, but I was afraid of the answer," Jeff said.

Chief told him that he had robbed the old man and had hurt him. It wasn't until much later that Jeff found out that Chief had killed the shopkeeper. He told Chief that he wanted no part in the robbery, he did not want any of the money and said he was going to call his mother to come and get him and Betty.

"My mother came to pick Betty and me up. She asked me what had happened and I told her that Chief had killed a shopkeeper. "I didn't take any of the money and I did not go inside the store," he said. "I told her that I would never hurt anyone and I never really thought that Chief was going inside that store to rob it. Mom said that she would take us to South Carolina and hide us out until she could think of what to do.

"My mother found us a small apartment within walking distance from the town. We didn't have a car and would have to walk to work. I found a job with Manpower and Betty got a job as a waitress not far from our place. For the next month we stayed there with Mom coming every week to bring food and just to visit.

"It was only a few weeks later that she told me that the police had questioned her about my whereabouts. They told her that they had Strouth in custody and only wanted me as an accessory to the robbery. It was then that I decided to turn myself in. I didn't think I would have to serve that much time for I had not taken an active part in the crime."

Jeff turned himself in to the Buncombe County Sheriff's Department and gave a statement without an attorney present. The detective from Tennessee had told him that he would not need one since he was only an accomplice. This was the first of many mistakes that Jeff was to make.

Chief had been caught and during his trial witnesses linked him to the murder. His girlfriend Barbara Davis testified that Chief had told her that he had done what he knew best. He had hurt the old man and slit his throat. She took police to the spot where they had buried his blood-stained jeans. Chief's friend, Jeff McMahan, told the jury that he got a call from Chief the day of the murder. Chief had told him that he had killed an old man in a robbery. Chief had gone to High Point, North Carolina, in the car that he had bought with the stolen money. Jeff McMahan said he saw the blood-stained jeans that Chief was wearing. Betty also testified that when she got in the car with Jeff and Chief that day she saw the clothes in the back seat. She also noticed the blood on the jeans that Chief was wearing and when she asked what had happened, Chief replied: "I had to hurt an old man, I slit his throat." The used car salesman testified that it was Chief that had given him the money for the old car that he had sold to him. He pointed Chief out as the one he gave the title to. Chief stood on the Fifth Amendment and would not clear Jeff. He told Jeff that he would tell the truth later on after their appeals ran out.

It didn't take the jury long in giving Chief the death sentence and he was taken to the Nashville prison.

"My mother went to a lot of attorneys to find one to represent me," Jeff said. "But they all said the same thing, that I should not have given a statement without an attorney present. The police did not have any evidence against me except the statement that I had given them. It would make my defense harder as I had admitted to being there. I was given a court-appointed attorney, James Beeler. He had never handled a capital case before and felt that he was not qualified to do so. Mom still wanted to get me another attorney. She had found out that they were going for the death penalty on me too."

Jeff was taken to Tennessee where he was put in jail to await the trial. The attorneys had wanted $100,000 to represent him and he knew that the family could not come up with that kind of money. Bond was set at $100,000 and even with a bondsman it would take $10,000. "My mother became desperate when she could not raise the money for an attorney and decided to break me out of this jail. It was not a successful attempt and the authorities decided to move me over to Brushy Mountain Prison in Knoxville where security was tighter.

"When my mother could not break me out and could not raise the money for an attorney legally she decided to write worthless checks. She was able to get some money by selling the house and the checks to hire Larry Smith of Asheville, North Carolina. He had never handled a capital case either, but Mom felt that he would be better than a court-appointed attorney. As it turned out this lawyer was worse than any that I could have gotten. All he wanted was the money. Mr. Beeler felt that I was innocent and did all in his power to represent me. But Larry was the lead attorney so what he said was what they had to do. Even though Mr. Beeler had never tried a capital case, I believe that he would have done a much better job than Larry did."

Jeff was tried in Greeneville, Tennessee. His attorney did not call on witnesses that had testified at Chief's trial that may have cleared him from getting the death sentence. The prosecution made it sound as though Jeff had needed the money and had gone inside the store with Chief. He never called the Fuller Brush manager to prove that Jeff was still selling in Kingsport and did not need the money. If he was short one week his mother would get whatever they needed. They were not told that Chief alone spent the money on a used car for himself. Barbara was not allowed to tell the jurors anything that Chief had told her about the crime, or that he had committed it alone. When Strouth was brought in, he would not tell the jury that Jeff had not taken part in the crime, and had not gone inside the store with him.

If Jeff had gone inside the store with Chief it would have made him guilty in the felony murder rule. If a murder is committed while a robbery is going on, then all present are just as guilty. It does not matter who actually committed the murder.

The jurors came back with a guilty verdict and the death sentence. "My mother was taken out of the courtroom by the sheriff because she yelled out during the argument. She was trying to tell the jurors that I had not taken part in the murder and the judge yelled for the sheriff to put her in jail. It tore me up to see the pain she was going through and I wished there was something that I could do for her."

During this time Betty had a baby girl whom they named Shirley Maria. She decided that she did not want to be a mother and was going to give it to the orphanage in Knoxville. "My mother talked to Betty and decided that she would raise Maria. She said that she would not allow my child to be given away to strangers. Betty just felt that she could not be a good mother, she couldn't take the responsibility. I felt sorry for her and I still love her today. Not everyone is cut out to be a mother."

Jeff was taken to Nashville where he was put on death row. Everyday is spent in an 8×10 cell which contains his bed and every item he owns and is allowed to have. The are only allowed out one hour a day to the yard for exercise. Noise is constant and loud, radios and TV blaring, each trying to outdo the other. Shouting goes back and forth between the inmates and the guards and the inmates. There seems to be so many people always around, yet each man is lonely.

"The routine stays the same day after day," Jeff says. "There are no activities whatsoever. You're always walking straight ahead without really seeing. There is always something missing. It's like there is a hole right through you. You can't figure out what it is, but you always have that empty feeling. All your eyes can focus on is tomorrow. You know tomorrow is only going to be a rerun of today but that doesn't seem to matter. You're always striving for that next day and putting another one behind you."

Jeff spends most of his time listening to cassette tapes. "My music is my last link to being on the outside," he says. "Through it I can go back in time and enjoy the good times over and over." When he isn't listening to his tapes, Jeff reads a good deal. He takes advantage of the hour a day in the exercise yard to get a breath of fresh air. The rest of the day is spent in the cell.

He knows that he is innocent and feels that one day it will be proven and he will get a new trial. He feels he certainly hadn't had a fair trial the first time around. During that first year he was alone. His mother and daughter and younger brother had to flee North Carolina because of the check charges against her.

"My sisters worked hard to pay off the charges against Mom and had the authorities sign a paper stating they would not prosecute her when she turned herself in. I didn't want her to come back because I knew what they had done to me and I knew they would give her a jail sentence. I didn't want my mother to be put in prison.

"She was lucky and received a year's probation. She was allowed to visit once a week with me. The first time I saw my daughter she was a year old. I can't tell you the feelings of love I experienced as I held her in my arms. She would put her arms around my neck and say, 'I love you daddy.' It was a three hundred mile trip one way from North Carolina to Nashville so Mom decided to move her and Maria over here to be able to visit me twice a week. I look forward to those visits and have watched my daughter grow up. She is nine years old now and so pretty. I couldn't have made it without their love."

Jeff's attorney, Larry Smith, was disbarred on perjury charges a few months ago and is no longer on the case. Jeff represents himself because the family cannot afford an attorney. While in prison the past nine years he has taken many Bible courses, gotten his G.E.D. and has taken an 18 month law course from the Blackstone School of Law.

All through the years his grandmother and grandfather have made the trip every other month to see him. They live on a pension and money is tight, but love for him keeps them coming every time they can. His sisters come when they can get off work. Now that his younger brother is

20 he also comes over when he can to visit. The inmates agree that it means a lot to anyone in the isolation of death row to be able to visit with their families.

"I guess the hardest thing for me is to know that sometimes the kids at school make fun of Maria about me. Kids can be cruel and I hate that she has to go through it. One day she put her arm around me and asked when I was coming home. How do I answer her?"

When people usually think of death row, they envision the likes of Charles Manson and other notorious mass murderers. They are taken aback to see that the men on Tennessee's death row are not that much different from people you meet every day. There is no crazed glint to their eye; no foam coming from their mouths. They are sad. And frightened. And they are human beings. The saddest thing about the death penalty is that innocent people are sometimes sentenced to die. There have been cases officially proven where the men were not guilty of the crimes with which they were charged. It was already too late for these men; they had been executed.

Twenty-Nine

Rose Williams — Mother

Rose Williams is a minister in the Church of God in Baton Rouge, Louisiana. During the week she works as a hospital supply clerk. She is the mother of three sons and one daughter.

"My son Robert was married and lived out on his own. He would get moody and had a lot of problems with drugs. When this happened in nineteen seventy-nine it was just a shock to all of us. We couldn't imagine that he would be involved in taking someone's life. But when I did get a chance to see him after he was arrested, he was like a different person altogether. He looked wild and I guess he was strung out on drugs. I had never seen him like that before. It was really heartbreaking. All we knew to do was to pray and trust in God. I believe it was this trust that brought him through the withdrawal. He didn't have any medical help or assistance. It just tore the entire family up and all we knew to do was give him our support.

"We did not have the money to hire lawyers like we needed to. We had to depend upon a court-appointed one. There was so much information that we were never able to get, still haven't gotten to the bottom of all it.

"Robert told us that he was shooting up on drugs. He and his wife and her uncle went to rob the grocery store. His wife had found him that night drunk and stoned and told him to get in the car with her and her uncle. They went to a grocery store and his wife sat in the car and he and Ralph went inside.

Robert was handed a shotgun and he went inside with the Ralph Holmes. They had ski masks over their faces. Robert held the shotgun on the security guard while Robert attempted to take the security guard's pistol. The shotgun went off and the guard was killed. Robert maintained the gun discharged accidentally. The gun was missing its firing pin, and other witnesses testified that it discharged accidentally later when he laid it on the ground.

They were caught a few weeks later and his wife turned state's evidence and was released. Holmes got life and Robert got the death sentence.

"My son said he never pulled the trigger and I believe him. We just couldn't imagine this happening, and yet we know when people are out there involved in situations like this, anything can happen. We just did the best we could and it was at this time we came into contact with the group, Southern Coalition on Jails and Prisons. We met Joe Ingle who was working against the death penalty. They gave us the greatest support of all. They worked real hard with us and did all they could to keep him from going to the chair. It was just something that in our state, they were anxious to get back to the executions. They really pushed it with my son.

"There were other cases where they knew definitely that the person had planned and committed a murder. These people did not get capital punishment. There was one case where the young man's mother and father were police officers. He had committed two murders at the same time and the district attorney was in support of helping him. This we could not understand.

"We searched the records and found time and time again where this was the case. Yet for my son they pushed for the death sentence. We do not support capital punishment. We feel it can't be justly administered. We don't believe this is the way to solve murders and killings. We believe there is a better way to correct this kind of problem. We don't believe we solve killing by killing.

"We believe there are other means we can take. We don't mean that they should go free and be out on the street. We believe they should be punished, but not capital punishment. This is why we fight against capital punishment. We have had members of our family who were killed and there never was a capital punishment in those cases. We never pushed for it. We didn't just decide this after Robert was convicted, this is what we believe.

"I'm not bitter, but it has made me sense the need to work hard to correct what is wrong with the system. I've seen so many people who are bitter and full of hatred because of their loved one's life being taken and this is not the answer. I think love and forgiveness and trying to work with people to help bring about a good relationship between each side is the answer.

"The only solution is to trust in God and pray to have forgiveness and not bitterness stay in our hearts. This is one of the things I prayed for during Robert's time, that God would help us not let bitterness and hatred come into our hearts. I can say that God answered that. Even with Robert, the last day we spent with him, his main interest was in talking to young people, and he said to get your life right with God. He told his son to make a good life for himself and not to make the mistakes that he had made.

"He said to remember the things they had been taught as children and to follow them. We spent all day long with Robert the last day. We were there till the early part of the night." Rose contacted the governor's office with a request; in the event the execution went through she wanted to watch. "I watched my boy come into this world and I want to see him go out of it," she said.

At the prison the Williams family and a handful of supporters prayed in the rain. They waited, always hoping that the governor would grant a stay to save Robert's life but none came. As Robert entered the execution chamber he told the executioners that "God has entered my heart and saved me." He pulled off his watch and said to give it to his 14-year-old son. He said, "Tell my children I love them. Tell them to live right."

In the cemetery over Robert Williams, the Reverend J.D. Brown said, "The deterrence for crime is not the chair, the deterrence for crime is Jesus Christ. Earth to earth, ashes to ashes, dust to dust."

Thirty

Dovie Page — Mother

Dovie Page was married for almost 22 years to Roy O'Guinn, but it ended in divorce. "Our son Kenneth is on Tennessee's death row. I started living my life for Jesus Christ after my divorce and moved back to Tennessee to live. My youngest children lived with me during this time. We had been in Jackson and I thought everything was going smooth. Of course we had the usual problems of never having enough money, but on the whole, I thought everything was going good. We had never had any big crisis in our family up to the time that Kenneth found himself in trouble with the law. I had eight children to start with, twelve grandchildren and four great-grandchildren.

"Kenneth was married and divorced before he was sent to prison and I haven't seen his kids since all this happened. He had three children and I was never allowed to see them. He divorced his wife, as they didn't get along very well, so things just weren't well between her and me either.

"When he first got into trouble I was shocked. I couldn't believe it then and I don't believe it now. They said he killed a girl he picked up in a bar. She had been there for a graduation party they said. It just didn't sound right.

"Kenneth was in Alabama when they discovered the body. She had been strangled with her own clothes. They notified all the little towns and cities near where the crime was committed. A detective came to me and showed me all kinds of pictures and told me that Kenneth was in jail for murder. He had a picture of Robert and said it was Kenneth. That was my other son, and I told him that was not Kenneth but Robert. He asked if I had a picture of Kenneth and if he could have it. I didn't think nothing of giving the law a picture and I gave him one.

"He turned around and used those pictures of my children and tried to get people to say that they were involved. We had court-appointed attorneys and they didn't do anything to help Kenneth. I think if Kenneth would have had different counsel, he wouldn't have gotten the death sentence. The victim's cousin got up on the stand and told how she was strung out on drugs that night and could have gone out with anyone.

"A dog catcher could have done a better job at defending my son than the lawyers he had. I thought he would have been found innocent. I was brought up to believe that you are innocent until proven guilty, but I found out it's not that way at all. There was no evidence linking him directly to the murder, none of the hair found on the girl was Kenneth's. They clipped hair from all over his body and none of it matched up with what they found on her nails.

"The only thing that put him in the place was the way they interrogated him and he signed some paper saying he was there. I don't know if he thought it was a confession, but he signed it.

"When the death sentence came down, it was hard to explain the way I felt. Seeing a judge who through the years knew us, and then when they picked the jurors, some of them said they didn't want to serve, he made them, I just felt it was all unjust.

"Kenneth knew I was upset and told me that there were appeals to go through and not to worry, but I was petrified. They wouldn't even let him touch me, and I know he's innocent no matter what.

"This new attorney that took Kenneth through the last appeal found some new evidence so hopefully we can get a new trial. I hope and pray that somehow those who are innocent will get out. If they were to execute my son, I hope he would die from a heart attack, than to be executed for something he didn't do. I know my son and I know he did not kill anybody. There's nothing that anyone can tell me or say, or even show me that would make me believe he was guilty. I would not believe it until Kenneth told me himself.

"This whole thing has made me bitter at the justice system that could do this. It's harder to prove you're innocent than guilty. I spent the worst time in my life in that courtroom watching the law being misrepresented. They weren't trying for the truth, they were trying for a conviction. You're lost before you even get started if you don't have the money for your own lawyers.

"People that really know me have stood by me. It's the strangers who, when they find out that I'm Kenneth's mother, act as if I have something catching. When it first happened, people would stand in groups and talk about Kenneth killing this girl. They never said supposed to have, they said he did kill. They tried him before the trial and found him guilty in the press.

"I pray that Kenneth has patience to last through the appeals. I pray that I will be able to stand up to all that faces us in the future. People don't know what we are going through. I can't see Kenneth very often, only like once a year when my brother takes me over to Nashville. I can't come by myself because I don't have a car to come in. I live alone and it's all I can do to keep myself going. I only get three hundred dollars a month and that's not enough to keep going.

"I feel there has to be a reason the Lord is putting us through this and one day I'll know why. I just wish the court could have seen that Kenneth was innocent and not messed his life up like that. I will rely on my faith that it will all come out all right. Before all this happened, I really believed there was justice but I don't feel like that anymore."

Thirty-One

Georgia Barber — Mother

Georgia Barber had six children to raise so there was never enough money to have extras in life. Her son Terry is on Tennessee's death row for the murder of Lora Smith. She says he is innocent of the crime for which he was convicted.

"I was married in nineteen fifty-five and Terry was born in nineteen fifty-six. We lived in Tennessee until Terry was a year old and then we moved to Illinois. We stayed there until nineteen eighty-five. Terry had a normal childhood growing up and never seemed to get into any trouble. He had a lot of friends in school. I stayed home with the kids, having that many kids, I kind of had to. My husband worked in a factory and we survived on what he made. I did go to work parttime once the kids were old enough, but it was kind of rough.

"My husband is disabled and has been for the past five years. He and Terry got along great all the time and there was never any harsh words between them. We moved to Ridgely, Tennessee, just a hundred miles from Memphis. We live in a small place there and never dreamed that anything like this could ever happen to us. It's just something you never dream of happening to you, but it sure does.

"After he was arrested for this crime, I was speechless and couldn't believe this was really happening. We had to get court-appointed attorneys because we didn't have the money to hire one. During the trial, I was so upset they had to carry me out. I just couldn't take it, there was so much happening all at once.

"The crime was investigated enough and I think our attorneys could have done better if they wanted to. Maybe if I had more money to give them, they would have done a better job. I think the outcome would have been better. I don't believe this attorney had ever handled a capital case before. I didn't know that much about the justice system.

"They put such a high bond on Terry that we couldn't touch it at all. I don't know why they do that, unless they wanted to make sure they stayed in there. I had two sons convicted of the same crime. I had to go through two trials and it was more than I could stand. They were trying to get the death penalty for both of them, but my youngest son was given a life sentence.

"They were going to try them together but then at the last minute decided to try them separately. They had different lawyers and a different judge and jury. They were out to get them both and they did. When this all came up, I almost lost my husband as his lung collapsed in June and again in August he was back in the hospital. He did go to the trials with me.

"For Terry's trial they were going to call me as a state witness and I couldn't be in the courtroom with my son. They finally agreed that I was going through enough and they didn't call me to the stand. Not until the end when I got up to plead with the jurors to spare him. I begged them to give him another chance. I told them that no one knew what it was like unless they had lost a child. I had lost one child at the age of five, and didn't want to lose another child too.

"I was just begging for mercy but we didn't find any in that courtroom. They took my other son to another place to have his trial. They offered him a life sentence in exchange for a guilty plea, but we decided that he was not going to do that.

"Our lives have been changed since this all happened. A couple of people in town kind of sneered their nose. They thought they were better than I was. Some of the people at work don't know how I cope and I tell them that it takes a willpower and a want-to. This isn't the end, I'll make it and I have the rest of the kids to look after. My husband is very sick and needs me to look after him. I have to be strong for all their sakes. I can't let it get me down. Sometimes it gets me feeling sad when I'm looking at pictures and I cry, but I'll make it.

"A lot of people won't talk about it thinking it will make me upset. I just live it day by day. I can't bear the thought that the state will kill my son. I don't get to see them very often as we don't have the money to come down here to Nashville. If it really comes down, I don't know what I'll do. I have to hold up for my other kids' sake and my husband's sake.

"I can't figure out why some of those people who really need the death sentence don't get it and then someone else gets it right off. The trial was only a week long and that's not long for a capital case. There was a case here at the same time that Terry was going to trial where a young boy killed his mother and dumped her body in the river. He was given life and he admitted to the murder and took police where he had dumped her. I can't see the fairness in all that.

"Terry never admitted to the killing, he said he didn't do it. My son-in-law was involved in the same case but he is walking free. He testified against Terry and my youngest son and was given freedom for his testimony. I don't think that is fair for one to walk free because he squealed on the others. He was involved the same as my sons were, and he should get the same.

"I've only been here once since Terry's been here. It's just too much to come over. The Reconciliation House here had a free weekend and I couldn't afford a motel room so when this came up, we decided to make the trip over here. We could stay there free and that's the only way we could come.

"I drive a little but wouldn't drive here in Nashville with all the traffic they have. These friends of ours will bring me again next year if they have the same celebration that they had on this Fourth of July."

Thirty-Two

Tina Mathews —
Grandmother

Tina Mathews was born in Wilder, Vermont. When she married Ernest Mathews, they lived in Concord, New Hampshire, for 20 years. After her five kids were grown, they moved to Asheville, North Carolina, to live. Ernest had heart trouble and was unable to work so they lived on a pension. Tina would work to supplement their small income. They felt the Southern climate would be best for Ernest's health and things were going fine until their grandson, Jeff, found himself in trouble.

"My two daughters and their families moved to Asheville along with my oldest son Michael. My middle son David and his family didn't care for the South so they decided to stay in New Hampshire. I would have loved to have all the children live in the same town as we did, but four out of five isn't bad.

"Jeff was my first grandchild. My daughter had him a few months after my youngest son Roger was born. They were raised together almost as brothers so they were very close. I never dreamed that anything so bad could happen in our family. A friend of Jeff's went inside the store and killed the shopkeeper. Jeff hadn't taken any of the money nor taken part in the crime, yet he was given the death sentence along with his friend. This so-called friend of his wouldn't get on the stand to tell the jurors that Jeff stayed outside in the car.

"I remember sitting in the courtroom, hearing the prosecution saying that Jeff went inside the store that day when there wasn't any proof to that effect. Jeff had waited outside and then turned himself in when he found out what had happened, but that didn't count to the police. Every word was cutting into me and I was afraid my husband was going to collapse from all the tension and security during the trial.

"My daughter had written hot checks to get an attorney when she found out attorneys wanted a hundred thousand dollars to represent Jeff. She sold her home and couldn't raise the money any other way. I was against her going against the law, but had to stand by her. She was doing what she thought was right to save Jeff's life.

"During the trial the prosecutor didn't put on witnesses that should have been called. The jury didn't hear all the evidence. It was just a kangaroo trial and there was nothing fair about it. I remember sitting in the courtroom along with Ernest, and watching the sheriff take my daughter out as she started yelling in the courtroom that Jeff was innocent and that Donald Strouth had already been convicted of the murder.

"You can't know the heartbreak of watching your daughter being dragged off to jail and your grandson sitting there fighting for his life. I didn't think my husband was going to make it through the trial for he is so emotional and loves his kids more than anything in the world. I don't know where I found the strength to keep on during all the emotional trauma of the trial. I knew that no matter what the outcome, my daughter and great-granddaughter would have to flee the state on the check charges. "As I listened to the judge I wondered why he was so unfair. He was the same judge that had sat on Donald Strouth's trial and he knew that Jeff was innocent, yet he wouldn't let anyone testify to anything that Strouth had said. This was unfair, for the jurors should hear all the evidence and not just the pieces that the judge and prosecution wanted them to hear. I believe that Jeff wouldn't have gotten the death sentence if they had been tried together.

"I could hear the jurors laughing in the room they were deliberating. They were deciding if Jeff would live or die and it was a party atmosphere. Why should they laugh at something like this? The bailiff had to go in a couple of times to quiet them down. This is the kind of people in the small town of Greeneville, Tennessee, that was to decide Jeff's future. I don't see how they could live with themselves afterwards knowing what they had done. They had to have known that Jeff wasn't guilty. The prosecution hadn't proven anything on Jeff. All the evidence was on Strouth. Jeff didn't have a chance in that place, they had found him guilty in the news media before they ever got to the courtroom."

Tina and what was left of the family still in the courtroom heard the verdict, guilty. The cries could be heard as the family held on to each other for support. Once back home, it was only a month before Ernest suffered a stroke and had to be hospitalized.

"Ernest and I used to go over to Nashville once a month to see Jeff. We would have to stay in a hotel for the night as we didn't know anyone over there to stay with. It was hard on my husband because of his heart condition. He worried over Jeff and our daughter Shirley. We would visit in a small room with others who were visiting their loved ones.

"Sometimes I would have to go over to Nashville by myself when my husband wasn't feeling very well. I would leave early Saturday morning and visit that day and then get up Sunday morning and visit. Then I had to drive the three hundred fifty miles back to Asheville, sometimes getting in at two in the morning and then getting up to work the next day. It was hard, but I had to do it. Jeff was such a good person and everyone had always loved him, it just tore me up to see him living in the hell that he had to live there on death row.

"It was a hard time and I lived on nerve medicine to exist. I had to be the strong one in the family. I had to worry about Jeff, Shirley and my husband. I don't know where I found the strength to go on, but I did. My daughter would call once a month at a pay phone because the police had mine tapped to find her. Her daughter Tina was paying back the checks and after a year, Shirley was ready to turn herself in.

"I had mixed feelings about that for I didn't trust the police or the justice system anymore, but she came in. She was lucky and only got a year's probation. Then she moved over to Tennessee in order to be near Jeff and visit every week. That gave us a place to stay when we did go over. We only had a little money and it didn't go far. It was just enough for the essentials of life.

"A lot of the past I have just blocked out of my mind. I don't want to remember all that went on so I guess I just blocked it all out. I had to keep Jeff happy, telling him that his mother was fine and how she was doing. He would worry so about her and his daugher. I don't think that anyone can understand the pain and shock that a person goes through during something like this. Unless they've walked in your shoes they don't know, and most don't care.

"Just when I thought things couldn't get any worse, my husband died of heart failure in nineteen eighty-four. It was an experience that I will never forget. We had been together for forty-five years and even though I knew his health was bad, I never expected to really lose him. He was my world and then in an instant, it was taken away from me. I often wondered why God was making me go through this hell that I was living in. All my children were with me, but nothing can ease the pain that I felt as I watched Ernest lying on the bed, his life slowly draining out of him. I guess I started drinking a lot during the weeks and months after he died, but it didn't make the pain go away, it just intensified it. The nightmare just didn't seem to be ending, instead it was growing worse all the time."

Then, Tina Mathews lost her mother and had to fly to Massachusetts to the funeral. This took a lot out of her and she wondered if anything else was going to happen in this lifetime for her to overcome.

"I still hate those people who sentenced Jeff to die. I can't forgive them for what they have done. I think they were all bucking to make a name for themselves and didn't care who they stepped on.

"I still go to Tennessee to visit Jeff but not as often as I used to. I guess I'm getting older and it takes so much out of me. I have my kids to lean on and they are wonderful, but nothing can erase the loneliness I feel when I sit here at night watching television. Sometimes I feel like Ernest is here with me, and Jeff is free. Then I realize it's all true: Ernest is gone forever and Jeff is still on death row. I have to be strong and pray that, one day, Jeff will be free to be with his family again. I will be strong and never give up.

Thirty-Three

Dawn and Tanya Perry — Daughters

Dawn and Tanya Perry are sisters who have a father on Alabama's death row. They were born in a small town in Alabama and lived there until Dawn was in kindergarten. Then the family moved to Knoxville, Tennessee, where they bought a small farm. The girls had a couple of horses and they were all happy. Their father, Eugene, owned his own construction company and did very well.

"I think it all started with income tax evasion, that my father began to get in trouble," Dawn said, thinking back on their lives. "My mother and father divorced and things were never the same again. I remember my father would take us girls a couple of times a month. We would go camping or out shopping, or just to a movie. We were very close and had a great communication between us. He was not there with me physically a lot, but the time we did have was quality time."

Dawn remembered her mother was the one who raised and fed them during those years. Eugene was sent to prison when Dawn was in the sixth grade and she was angry that he was not there to see her graduate. The resentment grew as she got older and she blamed him for his lifestyle that led to prison and being away from them.

"There was a lot of disappointment in high school and a lot of peer pressure," Dawn said. "I could hear people saying things as I walked down the hall and I didn't feel that anything my father had done should reflect on me. It wasn't my fault he chose to live the kind of life that was against the law and I shouldn't have to pay for his mistakes."

Dawn was 16 years old when she heard her father had been arrested on a murder charge. They hadn't heard from him in over a year and was shocked that this could be happening to their family. "I don't know all the details of how it happened but my father said he was not guilty of that crime and I believe him.

"My mother hadn't let me see my father for a couple of years because she felt he was a bad influence on me," Tanya said with a hint of tears in her eyes. "I was the youngest and I couldn't see how what he did would affect me. He's not a bad person and I just couldn't see what he did could affect the way I lived."

"I was at the trial but was not able to sit in the courtroom," Dawn said. "I had to testify in my father's behalf and it was hard. The jury just sat there like they were half asleep, like they could care less. They already had their minds made up that my father was guilty. There had been a lot of media coverage of the crime and everyone saw and heard about it. I believe that had a lot to do with his being convicted in the first place.

"The news media felt my father was guilty and said as much. Another man testified that he and my father committed the crime, and for his testimony he was given a life sentence while my father was sentenced to die. The jurors heard the news and read the papers so they thought he was guilty before they heard the evidence.

"While we were in the waiting room outside the courtroom the jury let out for a little bit, to rest. This one lady from the jury walked over to me and said to me, 'You're the Perry daughter, aren't you?' I told her that I was. She said, 'Well I just wanted to let you know that I don't know if he's guilty or innocent, but I'll sleep better knowing someone is convicted of it.' Tears came to my eyes and I said, 'I hope you sleep real good when you convict an innocent man.'"

It is common practice for the prosecution to offer a life sentence to one of the defendants in a murder trial if there isn't enough evidence for a conviction. Who is to know what the truth is when one testifies against the other for his life. Of course people will lie in order to live and give false testimony against the other person.

"I just don't understand how my father could have been convicted on circumstantial evidence. There was no physical evidence to link him to the crime but I guess the justice system can do whatever they want to do," Dawn said. "The jurors were not sequestered during the trial like in most capital cases. The judge just told them not to listen to the news or read the newspaper. I know those people watched the coverage on the news and probably read the newspapers also. They should have been sequestered so they could not have seen what the news media was saying. I just don't think that was fair."

"I was thirteen years old when my father was sentenced to die," Tanya said. "I was so nervous and I became hysterical and began screaming, 'No, no, you can't kill my father!' For a long time I was real hostile about it and if anyone called my Dad a murderer, I would feel like hitting them. Over the years I have come to accept the fact that he had chosen that kind of lifestyle. I don't approve of the things he has done in the past, but I love him. I hope one day he will get out and we can be together again."

Dawn married in 1984 and they moved to Nashville, Tennessee, where her husband was from. It didn't last very long and they divorced. She continued to live in Nashville as she had made friends and had a good job. During this time she would go to Alabama a few times a year to visit with her father. Her resentment was growing all the time even though she wasn't aware of it at the time.

"I had a hard year from nineteen eighty-six to nineteen eighty-seven where I didn't write to him or anything," Dawn said. "I had a lot of anger and resentment and I would think back to when I was growing up. He was never there except the couple of times a month he spent with us. I had basically given him all the credit and hadn't give my mother any. She is the one who clothed us and fed us. It just seems like he could have made choices that could have made our life together better.

"It was quality time when he did spend time with us, but it wasn't enough. I would hear my friends talking about what their fathers had done with them and I felt resentment. I just wouldn't write to him during this time until I sorted my feelings out.

"He would write to me during this time and lay a guilt trip on me for not writing and I would think, 'Where have you been all my life? Don't make me feel guilty for where you're at.' I was just going through a bad time. Then, last year I got a new job and bought a new car and I decided to go to see him. I knew I would have to talk to him and tell him what I was feeling and why I blamed him for not being there when I needed him. I was just mad that he was on death row."

"The first fifteen minutes of our visit, we both just cried. I didn't know we wouldn't have a contact visit and it totally shocked me when I walked in the room. There was a glass between us and we had to talk through a slot in the glass. I loved him, but I was angry. I wanted to let everything out. I had never told him before how I felt. It was a big block to me. I shouldn't have waited a year to do this and I felt sorry now that I had wasted that time.

"He asked me what was wrong with me and why I hadn't written him. I told him that I had gone through a lot of bad times. I had so many confusing thoughts just tugging at me like a tug of war that I didn't know how to feel. Should I love you, should I not love you. I was just so confused at this time. I told him that he was wrong to write me those letters making me feel guilty for not writing.

"I told him I loved him regardless of whether he did it or didn't do it. He always said he wasn't guilty of the crime that he was convicted of but if he did do it, he's still my father and I love him."

Tanya spoke up and said that she also had trouble with the noncontact visits. "I still haven't been able to put my arms around his neck and hug him like I did when I was younger. That really affects me a lot. I don't like looking at him through a glass and not being able to kiss or hug him. I just don't think that's right no matter what they think he did. When we go to visit with him and are ready to leave, we put our hands together on the glass and meditate and pray together. It's all I can do to walk away when the time is up."

Dawn and Tanya visit their father as often as they can make it down there. With the high cost of motels and food, it isn't as often as they would like, but they do make it every other month. "It's not like here in Nashville where they have Reconciliation House," Dawn said. "That is where the families of prison inmates can stay free of charge while they visit their loved one. For some of the people that is the only way they could ever visit. We would be able to visit more often if Alabama had the same thing down there.

"People aren't very nice to me because my father is on death row. A lot of people can't handle it and don't want to get to know me. I tell them the truth about where he is. That is why the Separate Prison organization here has really helped me. It's a place where we can talk about what is hurting us and know that all the women there will understand. They all have a loved one in prison and know the loneliness and the despair that I feel sometimes.

"When I hear they have set a date to kill my father, it scares me to death. The courts set an execution date while they hear the arguments. It is the attorneys that have to file a motion to have it stayed until the courts rule on the appeals that have been submitted. It's scary to know that one day the appeals will be over and the state really will murder my father. This is just not fair, for no one has the right to say my father should die. They are just as guilty of murder as they think my Dad is and I only hope and pray that one day he will be free to be with us."

Thirty-Four

Shirley Dicks — Mother

I remember the day I got a call from my oldest son, Jeff, who lived in Kingsport, Tennessee, with his wife, Betty. He sounded scared and asked me to come to Tennessee to pick them up, saying he would tell me what it was all about when I got there. I lived in Asheville, North Carolina, over the mountain from Johnson City where they were waiting in a hotel. I felt dread as I drove the miles over the winding, twisting road that led me to my son. When I finally pulled into the hotel, I could see Betty waiting for me and I followed her into the room to where Jeff was waiting. As soon as I saw his white face, I knew that something bad had happened.

Jeff told me how he had been driving around with his friend, Donald Strouth, who was also known as Chief. Strouth had instructed Jeff to pull over in front of a used clothing store, and then said that he was going to rob it. Jeff thought he was joking and waited inside the car, never dreaming that Chief would actually go inside and hold it up. When Chief came out with blood on his jeans, Jeff knew that something had happened. It wasn't until hours later that Jeff found out on the news Chief had gone inside and killed the elderly shopkeeper and stolen two hundred dollars.

All Jeff could think of was to get away from Chief, so he called me to come and get him and Betty. He refused to take any of the robbery money that Chief offered him. He wanted nothing to do with the crime.

I moved Jeff and Betty to Greenville, South Carolina, until I could decide what to do about it. I knew hiding them was wrong, but I was afraid of Jeff being put in jail. I would just have to think of some other way to handle things. After finding them an apartment and seeing that both of them had jobs, I went back home to think about all that had happened.

About a week later five detectives came to the Holiday Inn where I was a cocktail waitress. There, they questioned me for six hours in the back room, sometimes shouting loudly at me to tell them where my son was hiding out. Detective Keesling was a tall, hard-looking man who told me that if the police should find Jeff, they would shoot to kill. He assured me that they only wanted him to come in and be tried as an accessory to a robbery. They had Chief in custody and knew that he alone had killed Mr. Keegan. I told them that I was not going to tell where Jeff and Betty were, but that I would tell Jeff what they had said and if he wanted to turn himself in, then I would let them know.

As I left the motel that night my knees were buckling and I was afraid I would not make it to the car. Tears blinded my vision; I could barely see the road as I drove. As I screeched to a halt in front of the house, I screamed to my husband, Nelson. I began telling him what had happened, crying all the time and hardly taking a breath. He assured me that the police were right, that Jeff should come in and take his punishment, but there was something about the way the detectives had treated me that made me leery. I just had a feeling that something wasn't quite right. I wanted to trust Nelson and the police, but just couldn't.

I called Jeff the next day to tell him what had happened. He said that he wanted to come in for he was not guilty. He had taken none of the money from the robbery and had stayed in the car, and he was willing to come in and face the charges.

To our horror, when Jeff turned himself in, he was charged with murder one. Fear overwhelmed me; my mouth went dry as I asked the detective why he was charging Jeff with murder. I started crying and reminded him what he had told me, that Jeff would be charged with being an accessory to a robbery. Detective Keesling told me that the charge would be changed during the trial. Jeff gave a statement, without an attorney present, that he had been there with Chief and had waited in the car.

Jeff was taken to the jail in Blountville, Tennessee, not far from Kingsport. I went there to find an attorney that had handled a capital case before. Each attorney that I went to told me they would need a hundred thousand dollars for representing him. The fact that Jeff had given a statement without an attorney present was going to make it hard for a lawyer to represent him. An attorney would never have let Jeff say that he was at the scene. The police had no evidence linking Jeff to the crime.

As I drove home that night, I wondered how I was going to raise the kind of money that was needed to insure Jeff a fair trial. I felt as if I hadn't slept in a month and all the news I had heard only made matters worse. We had a new home but had very little equity, so I knew that selling it would not bring enough money. I would have to borrow it somehow. My husband, Nelson, was home and I told him what I had found out about the cost of a good attorney. He told me that Jeff would be given a court-appointed one and that was good enough. He didn't seem worried, and I started yelling at him that he didn't love Jeff. "I will raise the money with or without you," I shouted, running to my room.

Betty was living with me and my other three younger children. She was expecting a baby in August. I had found out that I was also pregnant and didn't know where it would all end. How would we cope? The whole world was crashing down on top of me and I didn't know where to turn for comfort.

In the weeks that followed, I worked two jobs to raise the money to find legal counsel. In the meantime, Jeff was appointed James Beeler from Kingsport. He had never handled a capital case before and he looked worried as he explained what was going to happen. He said Jeff's statement would be used against him and that he should never have been allowed to give one. All I knew of the legal system was from watching Perry Mason on television and the bad guy always got caught and the innocent one was set free.

Mr. Beeler said the state was going for the death sentence for Chief and Jeff. I felt faint and had to blink back the tears. This was a nightmare I was having and soon I would wake up to the normal day to day living. But this nightmare went on and on. I knew I could not afford a good defense attorney, so I decided to find witnesses who might clear Jeff.

Betty and I went to Kingsport to the scene of the crime. I began to question the people in the stores directly across the street from where Jeff had waited in the car. Suddenly, a policeman came over and told us to leave town. I tried to tell him that I was only trying to find someone who could testify that my son had waited inside the car that day. But again he yelled at us to leave town and not return.

Instead of leaving town, we went to the hotel and there I called the local television station. I told them what had happened and they sent a television crew out to interview me. I told them I needed to find someone who may have seen Jeff sitting in the car that morning. I gave them a picture of Jeff which they flashed on the screen as I talked into the camera. That night we saw it on the six o'clock news. It was supposed to run at ten o'clock, but I got a telephone call from the man at the television station. He said he was sorry, but so many people had called in and said they did not want the mother of a murderer to be pleading for her son, that they would not run it again. The people of this town had already tried my son and found him guilty before he even came to trial.

The next morning we drove back to Asheville. I was discouraged and could do nothing but cry. How could I save Jeff when they all thought him guilty? My pregnancy was making me sick all the time and I had to take care of the other children. Nelson was always there, but I could not talk to him about my feelings. He just said that everything was going to be all right. I heard that phrase over and over until I was ready to scream.

Chief's trial was held in Kingsport and they needed Betty to testify against him. The first to testify against Chief was his girlfriend, Barbara Davis. She told how Chief had come to her place of work that day in a car. She asked him how he could afford the car since she knew he hadn't had any money that morning. He told her he had robbed the shopkeeper and slit his throat.

I felt sick listening to her testimony, but also glad that the jury was hearing how Chief alone had committed the murder. It never dawned on me that Jeff would have a different jury and they would not hear all this evidence. Little did we know that the prosecution had planned it this way. By trying them separately, Jeff's jurors would not hear all the evidence. Had they been tried together, Jeff would not have gotten the death sentence. They wanted to make an example of him.

Barbara also testified that Chief called her to pick him up when his car broke down. When she got there, he was still wearing the blood-stained jeans. Barbara told him to rip them up and bury them in the woods. She later took police to the spot where the jeans were buried, and they were used as evidence.

While listening to the testimony, I saw Chief look back at me with a smirk on his face, and again I felt faint. I felt the evil coming from him and I shuddered. Jeff had been so naive to befriend this boy, but he had told me that Chief wasn't bad, he just didn't have a family who loved him.

The next to take the stand was Jeff McMahan, a friend of Chief's who lived in High Point. He testified that Chief called him the day of the murder and asked him to meet him at a convenience store. When McMahan arrived, he saw blood on Chief's jeans and Chief confessed that he had killed an old man in a robbery, and that his partner had froze up on him and waited in the car.

I was beginning to feel better now that I heard McMahan's testimony. Surely they could not give Jeff the death sentence when so many people had told how Chief alone did the crime.

The next to testify was Betty. She told how Chief and Jeff had picked her up that day and she had asked Chief how he had gotten blood on his hands and jeans. He told her that he had slit a man's throat.

The used car salesman also testified that it was Chief who paid two hundred dollars cash for the used car.

That night at our hotel, Betty brought McMahan in and I asked him if he would testify at Jeff's trial. He said that the state was paying his week's wages and his hotel room. I told him that I would do the same thing if he would just testify at Jeff's trial about what Chief had told him. Offering him money, would be one of the many mistakes I was to make.

It didn't take the jurors long to come back with the guilty verdict and the death sentence. Chief didn't say anything, just looked back at his mother in the courtroom. I looked up and saw Detective Keesling looking at me with a self-satisfied grin, and I had a sinking feeling. Suddenly I just knew; they were going to do the same to Jeff. I felt stifled; the walls were closing in on me. I had to leave the courtroom and ran outside to get some air.

I decided that there was no way I could raise the kind of money I needed to hire a good attorney. I was desperate and time was running out. The jail they were holding Jeff in was a small place that only had two guards there during visiting hours on Sundays. I thought that the only way to save his life was to break him out of jail. When I told Nelson what I was planning to do, he looked at me as if I had lost my mind. There were times when I wondered if I had.

"You're crazy," he yelled. "You're going to be sitting up there with Jeff. You can't get away with something so ridiculous. What if someone gets hurt?"

I assured him that we were not going to use bullets in the gun. I had a small .22 pistol that I carried in the glove compartment of my car when I traveled. Sometimes I would go 1000 miles to New Hampshire to visit relatives. Only the children and I would go, so I felt comfortable knowing that I could scare off anyone if my car broke down. I had never bought bullets for the gun as I was afraid one of the children would accidently set it off.

I know now that I was bordering on insanity. Fear was driving me to do things no sane person would contemplate. At the time, it seemed the only answer. Nelson told me that he would not help in my crazy plan. I figured I would need three other men to hold the guards in the jail until Jeff and I had left. But how was I going to find someone to help me?

Betty and I went to the roughest bar in Asheville. We were scared to death just seeing all the hard-looking people inside. We sat down, and a couple of foreign-looking men came over to the table. They didn't speak English well but it was evident they were trying to make a pass. I asked the one sitting closest to me if he wanted to make some money. I had saved three thousand dollars and I figured that would be enough. He said sure, but when I said I needed some help in a jailbreak, he looked at me as if I were crazy. Together they got up laughing and yelling at the others in the bar what I had asked him. This wasn't going well. Betty and I got up and quickly walked to the door and all but ran to the car.

How do you go about finding someone to help I wondered. I was beyond all reason now, and even my family was trying to talk me out of it. No one was going to kill my son, I vowed, not while I was alive. I did find someone who said he would help me. Instead, he went to the police with my plans, and when we visited the jail the following Sunday, there were guards and police everywhere. We had noticed a state police car following us from the North Carolina border, all the way to Blountville, but didn't know what was going on.

When we went inside the jail for our visit, there was a huge female guard. She could have been a lady wrestler, and I noticed that she just kept staring at me. I was beginning to feel nervous. I knew something was going on. The atmosphere was too quiet, not like it usually was. When we left the jail, we noticed that the police car was again following us back to the North Carolina border. It wasn't until we saw the newspaper the next day, that we knew what had happened.

"Deputies head off planned jailbreak," I read. They said that ten extra deputies spent seven hours stationed around the jail. They had increased security because someone had tipped them off about a jailbreak that was to occur during the visiting hours. They said that Jeff Dicks was the center of the attempt and as of yet no arrests had been made.

They moved Jeff to Brushy Mountain Prison where security was tighter and not many people had escaped. Now, I knew that the only way Jeff had of winning was to hire a competent attorney. It seemed as if everything was going from bad to worse but I had to keep trying, I had to hold up and stay strong.

I put my house up for sale, but knew it wouldn't bring enough money. Day after day I thought of ways to get money, and finally decided that I would write fraudulent checks. I would buy merchandise and then take it all to the flea market and sell it. It seemed to be the only answer. I just could not think of a legal way to raise the kind of money needed to defend Jeff. It was wrong to put such a high price on representation, and I cursed myself for not being wealthy.

I went to another city and opened a checking account using a different name. I knew what I was doing was wrong, but at the time, I didn't care what happened to me, if I could only get the money Jeff needed. Next, I got a driver's license using a phony birth certificate and waited for the checks to come in.

The first store I went to, I placed the items on the counter. My mouth went dry, and I was shaking as I wrote the check. I just knew everyone was watching me and that I would be caught at any minute. The salesclerk just smiled and gave me the bag. Quickly I ran outside, my heart pounding in my chest. I had made it. But at the next store the clerk questioned me more closely. He wanted to see more identification. I told him that I didn't have any on me, and that I would come back later, but he called the manager over. I didn't wait, but ran out of the store and sat in the car for five minutes until my breathing was normal again. For weeks I went from state to state opening bank accounts and buying merchandise.

Back home again I felt safe, but I was getting weary. All the traveling back and forth was beginning to have its effect on me. I was tired and had lost weight even though I was five months pregnant. I started crying over everything and just didn't know what to do. Nelson tried to help me, but I pushed him away. He didn't understand my feelings. I loved Jeff and knew he was going through hell in prison. I had found out from a guard that another guard had thrown hot boiling water on him as he sat helpless in the cell. Another guard, when taking Jeff to the hospital, put a pistol to his head and begged him to make just one move so he could save the taxpayers the money of a trial. I felt so helpless and didn't know anymore what to do or where to turn.

The days we went up to visit Jeff were the hardest. He had gotten so thin that he looked like a skeleton. His eyes were dull and sunken in his face. It just tore me up to see him like that. We could not hug or kiss, but had to talk through a small hole in the door. In order to hear, you had to put your ear to the hole and listen, then look up to talk again. I couldn't say anything, just cry. Hard as I tried to hold myself together in front of Jeff, I couldn't do it. My heart was breaking, and I couldn't control my emotions. I wanted to kick the door down, and take him away with me. Each visit he looked at me worriedly and said he was doing fine. I knew he was only saying that to ease my mind, but I knew differently. He was being mistreated and I was helpless to help my son. I prayed to God to please spare his life, he was a good boy, he had just been in the wrong place at the wrong time.

My oldest daughter, Tina, was working and she would give me all her money to help Jeff. She pleaded with me not to do anything else against the law. She was afraid that she would lose me too, and she could not bear that. I knew the pain I was causing my other children, but I was helpless to stop. I had one thing on my mind, and that was to save Jeff, no matter what I had to do. I explained to the kids that what I was doing was wrong, and I knew sooner or later I would have to pay for my crimes. Deep within me, I felt it would be worth it to be able to hire an experienced attorney for Jeff's defense. That's all I could think of—ways to get money. I couldn't eat or sleep and it became an obsession to me.

My grandmother lived in Massachusetts and I knew she had a Visa card. She had good credit and her limit was high. I decided to travel the thousand miles and steal it from her to buy more merchandise. I knew she would not have to pay the charges once she reported it stolen.

I visited with my grandmother for two days and had her Visa card in my wallet when it was time to leave. I felt guilty, but again I rationalized it by saying she would not have to pay the money back. I would have to face the guilt once it was known I had stolen the card. Still, I wondered if there wasn't another way, but if there was, I couldn't think of it. I left Nana's that day feeling terrible, physically and mentally, yet determined to get on with the buying of merchandise.

I hadn't gone far, when I started bleeding. I checked into a hospital, and lost the baby that night. Nelson flew in to be with me, and I signed myself out the next day. I had to start buying again, that's all I could think of. Time was running out.

Barely able to stand, I went to the first store and used the card. My knees kept buckling under me but I had to go on. All the way to Asheville, I stopped at store after store.

Betty had a baby girl, whom they named Shirley Maria, after me. We called her Maria though to avoid confusion. She was a beautiful little girl and as I held her, I thought of the child I had lost. Pain filled me and I blinked back the tears and cuddled her close.

The warden gave us permission to bring Maria to the prison for one hour. We would visit in a room with a guard present. At last we could give Jeff a hug and kiss. They also said we could bring in a camera and take some pictures of them together. I watched as Jeff very tenderly held his daughter. I saw the love and pride in his face and I knew the feelings he was having. He would want to protect his child, just like I was trying to protect him. When we left, I gave him a big hug and thought my heart would break as I felt his bony body close to mine. He was suffering, and I couldn't do anything for him. I would have gladly taken his place if I could have.

My family kept telling me to let the justice system work, that I was going to get myself in so deep that I would be in prison along with Jeff. But nothing they said could penetrate my mind. All I could see was the state trying to murder my child. I loved him and I would die before I would let anyone kill him.

My unlawful pursuits finally caught up with me in a small town in North Carolina. The clerk suddenly said she had to call the card in. I knew they didn't call the cards in if the amount was under fifty dollars, so I knew she suspected something. I told her never mind, that I didn't want the merchandise, but she was already on the phone. I ran out of the mall. Just as I was getting to my car, I saw the security car come flying around the corner and stop in front of the store. That marked the end of the credit card buying.

With the U-Haul full of merchandise, I went to Florida each weekend to the flea market then came back to visit Jeff on visiting day. Life was a roller coaster with no end in sight until I was able to hire an attorney in Asheville. His name was Larry Smith and after telling him the facts, he assured me that Jeff would get probation. I told him how I was getting the money and said I would send him a money order every weekend from Florida.

It was at this time Betty decided that she was going to give the baby up for adoption. She felt she was too young to raise the child and didn't want the responsibility. I told her I would adopt Maria. I had the attorney draw up the papers and she signed them.

Larry had given me hope which I clung to desperately. Mr. Beeler, the court-appointed attorney, was hesitant to tell me that Jeff would only get probation. He felt that Jeff would get time, a lot of it, but would not comment further. I felt uneasy and the fear was still there as much as I tried to push it aside. The trial was scheduled for February 5, 1979.

Larry explained that anyone testifying at a trial would have to sit outside the courtroom. Since I was going to get on the stand, I would not be allowed in. The jurors were finally picked, but they excluded all those who said they were against the death sentence. I felt weak and scared and knew Jeff was in for a big fight. I asked Larry where McMahan was and also the Fuller Brush manager. I had given him the telephone numbers so he could call them as witnesses. He told me he had everything under control and not to worry.

The prosecution brought in Chief's blood-stained jeans and tried to make the jurors believe Jeff had worn them. After questioning from Larry Smith, they conceded the pants were the ones Chief had worn. They said that Jeff was not working and needed the money from the robbery. Larry never called Mr. Clayton, the Fuller Brush manager, to disprove it.

Barbara Davis was called to the stand and with the jurors out of the courtroom, the judge told her she could not tell anything Chief said to her about the crime. It was called hearsay evidence and was not admissible. She could not tell the jurors how Chief had said he slit the man's throat, or that he had spent all the money on a used car.

I was getting tired of sitting outside and hearing about the testimony from family members. I asked Larry when he was going to call me to the stand. "I decided not to call you," he said. "I think you would fall apart and that would look bad for Jeff."

Larry didn't call on Betty and didn't put on much of a defense. The jurors had not heard half of the evidence. Mr. Beeler said he would have called on McMahan and the Fuller Brush manager but he was not lead counsel so had to go along with whatever Larry said. I was really worried now, the trial was over and it was time for the closing arguments. We would be allowed in the courtroom for that part of the trial and I sat down with my family.

The prosecution began by saying that Jeff and Chief had both gone inside the store that day and slit Mr. Keegan's throat. I jumped up in my seat and began yelling it was not true. I wanted the jurors to know that Jeff had not gone inside with Chief that day. On and on I went. Through a fog, I could hear the judge rapping his gavel and telling the sheriff to put me in jail.

I was put in a room with two other girls. From my cell I could see the room where the jurors were deliberating. I could hear their laughter and felt rage surge through my body. My son's life was at stake and it was as if they were laughing about it. The hours ticked by as I sat by the window watching, and waiting.

I heard footsteps coming to the room and my heart stood still. It was Mr. Beeler, and I walked slowly over to where he stood waiting for me. I couldn't read his face, but when he said, "I'm sorry," I screamed. Jeff had been found guilty of murder. I covered my ears and backed away from the door crying. The girls put their arms around me but I couldn't be comforted. The next part of the trial was to decide if Jeff was to get life or the death sentence. Again I waited by the window watching the jury room. I wanted to plead with these twelve people to please have mercy for my child. Where was God, I wondered. How could he let this happen?

Suddenly the back door of the courthouse opened and I could see my daughter, Tina, coming slowly out in the yard, her head bent low, her long brown hair covering her face. I knew in that instant the jurors had given Jeff the death sentence. Time seemed to stop, and I couldn't catch my breath; darkness was coming over me.

"No!" I screamed over and over. "You can't do that to my son. He's innocent! You can't send him to die. Oh God, no!" The screams went on and on as I held on the bars. The room was spinning around and around. I could hear my mother's voice yelling up at me to hold on. She was begging me to stop, saying we would fight it, but I had no mind left and the screams continued.

The door opened and my mother and a nurse came in. She gave me a shot and then I went off into darkness. The next morning, the guard came up and told me I could leave if I promised to be quiet. I agreed and was led down to the sheriff's office. There my family was waiting and we were told to leave Tennessee and not return.

A police car escorted us to the city line and one of the officers came over to the car. He told me that he couldn't believe Jeff had gotten the death sentence. He had been in the courtroom and heard all the testimony. He said he was sorry, but he had a job to do.

I knew I would have to leave North Carolina with my two youngest children, Trevor and Maria. The state marshal had come during Jeff's trial to question me about the checks and the credit card. I was supposed to come to his office as soon as I came back to Asheville. Jeff had been taken to Nashville where death row was located and I would not be able to see him.

Nelson was going back to New York and would take our daughter Laurie with him. She was sixteen years old now and did not want to go on the run. Becuase of all the turmoil we had filed for divorce and it was almost final, but Nelson told me to call if I ever needed anything.

I kissed my parents and daughters goodbye. We were all crying and I said I would get in touch with them as soon as I was settled. Now, I had lost Jeff, and also my family. I was alone and thinking of just ending it all. I couldn't do that, my mind kept telling me. I had Trevor and Maria to think of and the rest of the family. They all loved me and I couldn't do that to them.

Texas was the first place that seemed to be friendly enough, and I found a trailer for us to live in. Calling my family before the police had the phones tapped, I gave them my phone number so they could call me from the outside pay phones. I knew it wouldn't be long before the warrants were out for my arrest.

I was only there for a month when I broke all the bones in my ankle. I was taken to the hospital where I had surgery to repair the damage and had to stay for two weeks. The surgery was painful but somehow I welcomed the pain. It took my mind off Jeff. My mother told me he was doing all right and they had driven the three hundred miles to see him. The F.B.I. had been to question Jeff about my disappearance.

For the next year I was in a cast and wheel chair. Trevor took care of Maria and did a lot of the cooking. I couldn't seem to get myself together and constantly wondered how Jeff was doing. I had gotten cassette tapes from him, sent by my mother in another state. I received a Mother's Day card from him, and I felt the tears starting as I read the words he wrote; "Mom, Tho I don't say it very often, I want to say I love you. I'm very lucky to have such a special mother. I wouldn't trade you for my freedom. Thank you for always being there for me. I've never been good at showing my feelings, but always know that I love you mom and you make me proud."

Finally, I called my mother and told her to talk to the F.B.I. and tell them I would turn myself in if they would guarantee that I could visit Jeff one time before they sentenced me. My daughters, Tina and Laurie didn't want me to come in. They had paid back the credit card charges, but were afraid I would spend years in prison. I knew I would have to face up to the crimes I had committed, and I could not go on any longer without my family. I had to see Jeff again, no matter what price I had to pay.

The F.B.I. agreed I could go to Tennessee and see Jeff if I came in. I packed up Trevor and Maria and we came back to North Carolina. I was taken to the courthouse and after waiting awhile, the officer came to talk to me. He said if I pleaded guilty, the judge would give me a fine and a year's probation. I readily agreed to this and was released.

The first time I saw Jeff was just great. I couldn't hold back the tears as I held him. He hadn't known that I was turning myself in because I didn't want to worry him. He looked down at me and said he loved me. How I loved this man-child of mine. He held his daughter and she didn't appear to be afraid of him.

For the next year, I traveled back and forth every weekend to visit Jeff. The trip took six hours each way and was tiring, not to mention the expense so I decided to move to Nashville to be near him. I found a small trailer and we moved in. This way we could visit twice a week with Jeff and get him out of his cell.

I wrote to F. Lee Bailey and all the famous attorneys I could find. I was trying to find one that could find a mistake in the trial and have his sentence overturned. Larry Smith was not longer our attorney. Since the trial, he had been disbarred for perjury. I found Bart Durham of Nashville. He took us back to the post-conviction hearing. The same judge and prosecution were there. Bart tried to convince the judge that Smith, as lead attorney, did not provide adequate counsel. I had to go on the stand and apologize to the judge for my outburst in the previous trial. I didn't want to apologize, because I felt the judge knew Jeff was innocent. He was the same judge on Chief's trial. Mr. Beeler said he disagreed with Smith's defense of Jeff because he did not subpoena witnesses that we had given him, and because he had put Jeff on the stand unprepared. Mr. Beeler said Larry did not discuss a strategy and he was not being made party to the case preparation. He said Larry Smith would not return his calls about the case, and that friction developed between them during the trial.

Others testifying were state's witnesses who said they were not interviewed by defense lawyers. Smith responded to those allegations saying no witnesses would talk to him and saying he could not find any beneficial witnesses. Larry said that I had offered money to McMahan to change his testimony. I felt like slapping him in the face as he stood on the stand and said that. I had offered to pay his way over and the hotel room and food. He could not afford to come over otherwise and I felt his testimony was important. I didn't want him to change anything he had already testified to.

McMahan got on the stand and told how he had talked to me. He said I offered him money to come and testify for Jeff. "I can only tell you what Chief said down at the bridge. And he said his partner froze up in the car. I don't give a damn whether she sends me the money or not. When he said froze up, that means the guy stayed in the car," he said.

Back in Nashville we waited for the outcome of the hearing. It came back upheld. The judge would not agree that Jeff should have a new trial. Bart said to keep my spirits up, that the fight was not over. He assured me that Jeff would get a new trial in the Federal level. I wanted to believe him with all my heart, but my head told me different.

The years went on and Maria was starting school. She had grown up suddenly and I felt a pang as she went off to her first day at school. We took pictures so Jeff could see things she was doing. He wanted to participate in her life as much as possible. She loved playing with him when she visited the prison, often making him carry her piggy-back around the small room in which we had our visits.

I started reading all I could on the death sentence, finding out how unjust it all was. I would see others on the row getting their sentence overturned, some who had admitted their guilt in the crime, but because an error had been made at the trial, their sentence had been changed to life. I was glad for the men, but sorry that Jeff hadn't gotten one yet. Here he was, innocent, and he was still on death row. Chief was up there, but still would not tell the truth and free Jeff.

Tina and Laurie would come over to visit with Jeff when they could get away from work and stay with me. I was lonely and hadn't made many friends. The first few people I talked to, I was met with disdain and fear when they found out my son was on death row. Children were not allowed to play with Maria once word got out. She began to have headaches and was ill a lot. It made me angry to know that people could be so cruel and take out their hatred on us. Mostly, I stayed inside and kept to myself.

Jeff had an execution date but we didn't know it because Bart had resigned from the case. I hadn't been able to keep up with the monthly payments so after five years, he just quit without telling us. Larry Woods, an attorney in Nashville who fights the death sentence, stepped in and stopped the execution.

The years have been tough, but I've found the strength to go on. I knew I had to be strong for Jeff and Maria. Without their love, I couldn't have gone on this long. I finally put Maria in our church school and the headaches stopped. She is at the age when she knows the state wants to kill her daddy and she wonders why.

I have met many new friends in a writing group that I started and hopefully have changed many people's ideas on capital punishment. These people have accepted me for what I am, and not judged me on what I've done. Our church members are also getting interested in the prison. I gave them inmates' names that needed someone to write them. Now a lot of inmates have found new friends through the mail.

I keep hoping and praying that one day God will let Jeff walk out of the prison a free man. Until that day, we will keep on hoping and praying.

Bibliography

Books

Amnesty International, *The Death Penalty* (1979)
Amnesty International, *USA Death Penalty Briefing*
H. Bedau, *The Case Against the Death Penalty*
H. Bedau, *The Death Penalty in America*
H. Bedau, *Death Is Different*
Racial Discrimination, Poverty and the Death Penalty by the Southern Prisoners' Defense Committee
V. Streib, *Juvenile Justice in America*
V. Streib, *Death Penalty for Juveniles*

Experts

Hugo Bedau is an expert on the innocent sentenced to die. He, along with Michael Radelet did a study and found 350 cases of people wrongfully convicted of a capital crime, and wrote the book, *Miscarriages of Justice in Potentially Capital Cases.*

Marie Deans monitors capital cases recruiting appellate attorneys visiting persons on death row. She is head of the Virginia Coalition on Jails and Prisons.

Watt Espy, expert on all the executions in the United States. He has researched every known execution that has been recorded and heads the Department of Philosophy at Tufts University in Medford, Massachusetts.

Joe Ingle, expert on capital punishment. He was nominated for the Nobel Peace Prize in 1989 for his work on capital punishment.

Richard Moran is a professor of sociology at Mt. Holyoke College and has written on the financial cost of capital punishment.

Patricia Smith is the associate director of the Georgia Association of Retarded Citizens. She was clemency attorney for Jerome Bowden, a retarded black man executed in Georgia.

Victor Streib is an expert on juveniles and women on death row. He is a professor at the Cleveland-Marshall College of Law at Cleveland State University, and the author of *The Death Penalty for Juveniles*, Indiana University Press.

Index